THE COAT MY FATHER GAVE ME

C. Isaac De Los Santos

DEDICATION

This book is dedicated to Rev. George De Los Santos and
Lydia De Los Santos. My parents, whose godly example have been
a light to my life and a blessing to my soul.

Acknowledgements

I would like to thank my parents who are now with the Lord, for their tireless encouragement and investment into my life. They practiced what they preached and made growing up in ministry a thrill for my brothers and me. They took no small steps of faith, only big ones and their reward is eternally in Heaven.

I thank my two elder brothers and their wives. Anthony and Lisa for their unending support of my ministry. They are an inspiration to me as they lead their family and their church toward great heights for God. Josh and Nelda for their great and generous investment into my life and ministry. Together we bear witness to the truths I tried to convey in this book.

I thank Dr. Jimmy Longoria for his investment as a spiritual father into my life, and the lives of countless others. He is a gift to the body of Christ and a friend to me. His humble example of spiritual leadership has been the ballast of the great Unified Pentecostal Local Churches.

I thank the Rev. Samuel Montoya, another Spiritual Father who saw in me potential for service to the body of Christ and gave me a place to exercise my gifts. He opened up the doors of foreign missions and trusted me with leadership when I was in my early twenties. He has been a true mentor and a friend.

I thank my Staff at the Bethel School of Ministry for helping me do in practice what is taught in this volume. Jake Flores who has been a true son in the faith, whose teachable spirit makes him an asset to my life and the body of Christ. Sandra Sandoval whose many gifts have been graciously placed at the Lords disposal, and whose spirit of excellence has made my work easy.

I thank the Elders and Members of Kingway Church for their prayers, support, and encouragement. They make it possible to extend ministry from Beeville and the ends of the earth. Together we will go far in the pursuit of the presence of God.

C. Isaac De Los Santos

Introduction

This was the last sermon I would preach for my father. Within three short months he would be in the presence of his Lord. I had been asked to preach on the occasion of his Pastors Appreciation Banquet, and I preached a sermon titled "The Coat My Father Gave Me." My father was a kingmaker, whose investment in his sons prepared them to serve God and their fellow man. He never enjoyed great notoriety, nor did he pastor a very large church. What he did do however was train countless people for ministry, and I am one of them. His example has motivated me in my life to be about the business of raising up a future generation of spiritual leaders.

This book is not an autobiography, nor is it a biography of my father. And although it will focus primarily on the life of the Patriarch Joseph, it's not a biography of Joseph either. Rather it is a study of the impartation which a spiritual father makes to their sons. It is a blue print from the text of Scripture on how a son is prepared for success. My father's example serves as the foundation for my life, and I trust that Josephs story will serve as a blueprint for yours.

Whether in ministry or in life, there is an important value to preparing the next man or woman who is going to assume the leadership role. Leaders who acknowledge this responsibility to prepare in advance for the day when they will leave the stage and another will assume their place. This book is a response to the great hunger that exists in the 21st-century for spiritual fathers and the important role that they play in the lives of their sons and daughters. In my life I have had the privilege of being mentored and fathered by great men of God whose character, integrity, and example have prepared me for the work of the ministry. I acknowledge that without their investment, my life would be very different and perhaps I would be starving as so many are today for the impartation that can only come about from the father.

I currently serve the Pastor of Kingway Church in Beeville, Texas and had the privilege of launching the Bethel School of Ministry in Kenedy, Texas nine years ago. One night in prayer I said to the Lord, "Lord why have you given me such a burden and desire to raise up sons and yet you have not given me a family of my own?" I'll never forget that moment so long as I live, as I believe God and his gentle response to me said, "Isaac, I have given you, and will give you many spiritual sons." I knew then that he was laying upon me the burden and responsibility of preparing sons for ministry to the body of Christ.

I pray that through this book someone else may be encouraged to embrace the call to mentorship. The responsibility for raising up spiritual sons falls not only on me, but on many servants of God. We must take seriously this responsibility and do what we can to prepare the next generations of leadership for adequate successful spiritual leadership

I believe that the life of Joseph offers us a blueprint for spiritual sonship, and I want to focus in this book on three aspects of Joseph's coat of many colors. You will discover that the coat of many colors is a treasure hidden in plain sight. For in it each member of the Godhead can be seen and known. In the coat of many colors we see the grace and favor of God the Father, the atoning sacrifice of Christ the Son, and the anointing of the Holy Spirit. Each weaves through this coat the elements needed to equip us for divine purpose and success.

Furthermore, the coat serves as a symbol of the impartation which fathers make to their sons both in the physical relationship and the spiritual. Thus I pray that this book will equally serve as a rallying cry to Spiritual Fathers who perhaps have neglected their God ordained responsibility and privilege.

Let us explore together the "The Coat My Father Gave Me."

Chapter One

The Birth Of A Dreamer

Then God remembered Rachel, and God gave heed to her and opened her womb. 23So she conceived and bore a son and said, "God has taken away my reproach." 24She named him Joseph, saying, "May the LORD give me another son." Genesis 30:22-24

The home of the Patriarch Jacob was the epitome of the dysfunctional family. The modern reality TV audience would have been glued to their screens watching the day-to-day strife of Jacob's little tribe. Jacob had four wives, that's right, four striving, contentious, jealous wives. Leah he married because of a trick his father-in-law played on the wedding day. Rachel he married for true love. Bilhah he married because Rachel was barren, and Zilpha he married when Leah bore no more.

From these women were born a variety of children, and with each child the wives strove to obtain the affection of their husband. But Jacob was a biased man when it came to his affection, and it was Rachel who he truly loved. He loved her from the first moment he met her. Yet by a twist of irony it seemed that providence had played a cruel trick on Jacob yet again, and the woman he loved most, was most barren. Rachel famously cried out to him and God saying "Give me children, or else I die." So grievous was her desire for children, that she would rather die than be childless.

One cannot fault her natural desire and anyone who ever dreamed knows the desperation which comes when a dream's fulfillment is denied. The desire to be fruitful is built into us by our Maker, and suppressing the desire for greatness has left countless dreams unfulfilled. Not only has the desire for fruitfulness been built into us, but it is our appointed destiny.

Jesus said "You did not choose Me, but I chose you and appointed you that you should go and bear fruit, and that your fruit should remain, that whatever you ask the Father in My name He may give you."[1] Fruitfulness is our God appointed purpose. His desire of us that we bear fruit, good fruit, and much fruit. In another place Jesus said "By this My Father is glorified, that you bear much fruit; so you will be My disciples."[2] Yet there seems to be in our day a great silence in the church regarding our heart hunger for God glorifying fruitfulness.

Often it's not that we are guilty of prayerlessness, but rather guilty of praying small prayers. How often we utter passionless little prayers that limit God's work in and through our lives. Are we unaware that He is willing to do great things for those who will pray prayers as big as God, for the glory of God alone.

It was John Knox who cried out "Lord, Give me Scotland or I'll Die." George Whitfield prayed "Give me souls, or take my soul." John Hyde earnestly beseeched heaven saying "Lord, give me souls or take my life." These are the types of prayers that defined past centuries, and must again define our own. If we hope to see our cities turned back to God we must pray Rachel-like prayers. If we hope to see the millennial generation salvaged from spiritual coldness and ruin, we must learn to pray as Rachel prayed.

---

[1] John 15:16
[2] John 15:8

The Desire for Increase

At the core of Rachel's prayer was a very natural desire for increase. The desire for increase is native to the culture of the Kingdom of God. An attitude which adopts contentment with mediocrity and apathy in spiritual barrenness is antithetical to the very nature of God's Kingdom. Jesus said "The kingdom of heaven is like a mustard seed, which a man took and sowed in his field; and this is smaller than all other seeds, but when it is full grown, it is larger than the garden plants and becomes a tree, so that THE BIRDS OF THE AIR come and NEST IN ITS BRANCHES. The kingdom of heaven is like leaven, which a woman took and hid in three pecks of flour until it was all leavened."[3]

The very nature of the Kingdom of God is increase, and everywhere that the Kingdom of God is received it grows and ultimately takes over. Isaiah spoke of the increase of the Messiah's government saying "Of the increase of his government and peace there shall be no end, upon the throne of David, and upon his kingdom, to order it, and to establish it with judgment and with justice from henceforth even forever. The zeal of the LORD of hosts will perform this."[4] Our King and His Kingdom are forever established in increase by the will of God.

The Increase of the Gospel Globally

We first see the remarkable increase of the Kingdom in the global expansion of the Gospel. What began with one man named Jesus, then grew to twelve, then seventy, then five hundred at his ascension, then 3000 at Peter's first sermon, then Judea, Samaria, Asia Minor, Europe, North Africa, and the world. In spite of edicts, persecutions, and deluding influences; the Gospel spread and invaded the world without firing a single shot. "The path of the righteous is like the light of dawn, That shines brighter and brighter until the full day."[5]

Like the first glimmer of daybreak announces the fullness of a glaring noon time sun, so the Kingdom of Heaven enters

---

[3] Matthew 13:33
[4] Isaiah 9:7
[5] Proverbs 4:18

undetected, and increases to a glaring revelation of the divine objective. Paul spoke of this to the Corinthians saying "But thanks be to God, who always leads us in triumph in Christ, and manifests through us the sweet aroma of the knowledge of Him in every place."[6] That ever increasing knowledge of Christ in every place is God's will and it is accomplished through us.

The Increase of The Gospel in our Hearts

To further illustrate the Kingdom's nature of increase we can observe the increase of the kingdom in the individual heart. When the kingdom entered your heart, it came in like a small seed or a pinch of yeast. But now it has taken over your life, it changed the way you think, speak, act and react. God's kingdom grows and dominates the whole of a human heart once it has been received. The conversion experience is only the first pinch of glorious yeast which enters the flour of a man's life. That pinch of glory soon rules and governs the whole man. Likewise that pattern is seen in many families, where the Gospel leavens enters a heart, and eventually grows to envelope every member of the family.

Recently we baptized a husband and wife in our congregation who had given their lives to Christ and were excitedly venturing into a life of faith. On the morning of the baptismal service I met with the candidate to discuss the meaning of water baptism. As we discussed their conversion experience, the couple shared with me the fact that they had come to Christ because of their children, their son in particular. I was surprised to learn that their fourteen-year-old son was the catalyst for their conversion, and through that young man the leaven of the Kingdom had grown to include his whole family.

I had the privilege of being born into a similar story. Four generations ago, my great grandmother Maria Escamilla was dying of a severe respiratory disease called Tuberculosis. My great grandparents, Fidel and Maria Escamilla, were not religious people, and had little notion of any spiritual insight.

A group of Christian couples who knew about my

---

[6] 2 Corinthians 2:14

grandmother's need, arranged for a gathering at one of their homes. The men went outside to play baseball, because my great-grandfather was a baseball coach, and the women went indoors. This gathering of women soon became a prayer meeting, and the pleas for divine healing were graciously heard in heaven. My great-grandmother was miraculously healed of Tuberculosis, and became a believer in Jesus Christ. Soon my great-grandfather was converted, and then their children, and grandchildren.

By the time I was born, the leaven of the Kingdom was the native soil of our family tree, and the legacy which we inherited for generations to come. I was born into a Christian home, and came to know Christ as a boy. In fact at age seven I preached for the first time in a church service, and became the fourth generation of ministers in my family.

It has been correctly said that God has no grandchildren, and no one is born converted. Yet the fact that the leaven of the kingdom came into my family four generations ago made all the difference in the kind of life our family leads today. You may be a first generation believer in your family and when you look around you may wonder whether you will ever win anyone in your family to Christ. Let me assure you that the leaven of the Kingdom is bound for increase.

This same pattern often occurs in the revelation of God's call on an individual life. He may give you snapshots of His purpose along a timeline of many years, and slowly as you yield to His will He manifests the full panoramic of his design.

The Increase of Israel

Furthermore we see the nature of increase in the nation of Israel. Under Joseph the tribe of Jacob entered Egypt with a mere 70 souls[7], and yet would depart in the Exodus being a nation of millions. Scripture states that "the sons of Israel were fruitful and increased greatly, and multiplied, and became exceedingly mighty, so that the land was filled with them."[8] It was this increase that

---

[7] Exodus 1:5
[8] Exodus 1:7

frightened Pharaoh and led him to fear the Hebrew tribe, saying:

"Behold, the people of the sons of Israel are more and mightier than we. 'Come, let us deal wisely with them, or else they will multiply and in the event of war, they will also join themselves to those who hate us, and fight against us and depart from the land.' So they appointed taskmasters over them to afflict them with hard labor."[9]

The psalmist would later declare "You removed a vine from Egypt; You drove out the nations and planted it. You cleared the ground before it, and it took deep root and filled the land."[10]

The Revelation of Increase

Absolutely everything that God establishes increases, and that is a powerful truth which we must appropriate by faith. We must walk daily in the revelation that increase belongs to us as we do Kingdom business. If you are a Pastor then you should believe that God will give your congregation increase on every level, for the advance of the Gospel in your city. If you are a campus missionary, then you ought to believe that God has granted you the souls of your classmates and expect to see increase for the glory of God.

If you are a Christian businessman you ought to expect that your business will increase for the progress of the gospel. If you are a Christian in the market place, you ought to expect that God has given you the wisdom and insight to impact the market place for the Kingdom of God. Increase is the inherent destiny of Kingdom citizens, and the revelation of that fact is an imperative in our day. I am persuaded that the only times the church fails to advance is when it fails to walk in faith and the assurance of its Kingdom agenda and Kingdom increase.

If you haven't noticed by now, I've used a word a half dozen times which is the key to kingdom increase at any level. The increase of the Kingdom of God cannot be built, manufactured, or

---

[9] Exodus 1:9-11
[10] Psalm 80

cajoled; it must be "received" by faith.

Jesus said "Truly I say to you, whoever does not <u>receive</u> the kingdom of God like a child will not enter it at all."[11] And furthermore the write of Hebrews stated that we have "<u>received</u> a kingdom which cannot be shaken."[12] The Kingdom of God must be received by faith in the heart of a believer which takes for granted that increase is the will of God and the pattern of God's work in the world. "Faith" is the coin of the realm, and increase is the agenda of our King.

The issue then lies with our inability to recognize this truth, or else with our unwillingness to believe that it applies to us. If you hope to do anything great for the Kingdom of God, you will need a revelation of divine increase and provision. The fact that we do not have a revelation of divine increase, accounts for the fact that they do not pray great prayer nor attempt great things.

The famed bible teacher Derek Prince stated that "God's abundance cannot be understood or appropriated unless it is revealed by God."[13] This principle is true in everything that we receive from God. We will never pray for increase unless we can see its availability in the spirit by faith. The Lord said to the prophet Jeremiah "Call to Me and I will answer you, and I will tell you great and mighty things, which you do not know." And in response to that he said "I will reveal to them an abundance of peace and truth." This revelation of divine abundance comes primarily in two ways.

First it comes as we call upon the name of the Lord. He said "call upon me" and "I will show you great a mighty things." The word "show" in the Hebrew is that verb "negad" which literally means "to make something conspicuously known."

God says to us, if you call upon me I will make known my will in a way that will be clearly manifest and undeniable. Further he says that calling upon him will lead to a revelation of His

---

[11] Mark 10:15
[12] Hebrews 12:28
[13] Prince, Derek. Gods Abundance Vol XVIII Issue 4

abundance. When you think about your life or ministry, do you think about lack, obstacles, and limitations? When you pray, to do pray only in reaction to your needs, or do you pray in light of the increase that you believe God has for you?

I have found that when I have my eyes on my circumstances, I do not pray great prayers. It's hard to believe for increase when lack is your focus. But I have also found that when my eyes are on the Lord, and his voice is clear in my heart, when I am walking in the revelation of his desire to increase his Kingdom through me, I not only pray bigger prayers but I do greater works. There is then a great challenge before us to keep our eyes on what has been revealed above and work towards that reality.

Secondly this revelation comes through our faith in God's word. No one should expect to do any great things for God, without faith. Without faith we know that it is "impossible to please God."[14] Yet with faith Jesus said that "all things are possible to him that believes."[15] Thus faith is an essential ingredient for increase.

The Promise of Increase

Let's look for a moment at what the scriptures say concerning increase:

Though your beginning was insignificant, yet your end will increase greatly. Job 8:7

He will bless those who fear the LORD, the small together with the great. May the LORD give you increase, you and your children. Ps 115:13-14

He changes a wilderness into a pool of water, and a dry land into springs of water; and there He makes the hungry to dwell, so that they may establish an inhabited city, and sow fields and plant vineyards, and gather a fruit of increase. Psalm 107:36-38

---

[14] Hebrews
[15] Mark 9:23

A wise man will hear, and will <u>increase</u> learning; and a man of understanding shall attain unto wise counsels. Proverbs 1:5

Also He blesses them and they <u>multiply greatly</u>, and He does not let their cattle decrease. Ps 107:36-38

Give instruction to a wise man, and he will be yet wiser: teach a just man, and he will <u>increase</u> in learning. Proverbs 9:9

Wealth gotten by vanity shall be diminished: but he that gathers by labor shall <u>increase</u>. Proverbs 13:11

Now Jabez called on the God of Israel, saying, "Oh that You would bless me indeed and enlarge my border, and that Your hand might be with me, and that You would keep me from harm that it may not pain me!" And God granted him what he requested. 1 Chronicles 4:10

Enlarge the place of thy tent, and let them stretch forth the curtains of thine habitations: spare not, lengthen thy cords, and strengthen thy stakes. Isaiah 54:2

Now He who supplies seed to the sower and bread for food will supply and multiply your seed for sowing and increase the harvest of your righteousness. 2 Corinthians 9:10

Then Isaac sowed in that land, and received in the same year an hundredfold: and the LORD blessed him. Genesis 26:12

I will run the way of thy commandments, when thou shalt enlarge my heart. Psalms 119:32

Thou hast enlarged my steps under me, that my feet did not slip. Psalms 18:36

The LORD God of your fathers make you a thousand times so many more as you are, and bless you, as he hath promised you! Deuteronomy 1:11

Without a doubt, the promises of God are endless toward His people, and His desire to increase them is well documented.

Wrong Prayers

Rachel's problem was not that she prayed small prayers, but rather that she prayed the wrong kind of prayers. Firstly, she prayed what I would call "disconnected prayers." She turned her prayers toward Jacob, who could not possibly hope to give her an answer. Her prayers were disconnected from the source of true provision, to a smaller and greatly inadequate substitute. Often if we are not careful, it is easy to put our sight on the wrong objects of faith. Trust in in Jacob while talking to God, has never yet secured an answer to prayer. This is because God is jealous about His glory, and will not share it with anyone, even a chosen servant like Jacob.

Jesus said "Abide in Me, and I in you. As the branch cannot bear fruit of itself, unless it abides in the vine, neither can you, unless you abide in Me. I am the vine, you are the branches. He who abides in Me, and I in him, bears much fruit; for without Me you can do nothing." In other words Jesus is saying don't get unplugged!

The only way to bear God glorifying fruit if to stay connected to the source of vitality and life. This is true for every sphere of life where we hope to bear fruit. Whether it be ministry or market place, in the context of the body of Christ or the home, we cannot bear fruit when our trust or faith is directed at anything other than God.

Secondly, she prayed with wrong motives. Scripture points out that "When Rachel saw that she bore Jacob no children, she became jealous of her sister; and she said to Jacob, 'Give me children, or else I die.'"[16] Her prayers were motivated by jealousy and not faith, which does not please God.

Matthew Henry states "The desire, good in itself, but often too great and irregular, of being the mother of the promised Seed, with the honor of having many children, and the reproach of being barren, were causes of this unbecoming contest between the sisters."[17] This contest led to envy and jealousy, which motivated

---

[16] Genesis 30:1

14

her prayers.

"Envy is grieving at the good of another, there is no sin more offensive to God, nor more injurious to our neighbor and ourselves. She considered not that it was God that made the difference, and that though, in this single instance her sister was preferred before her, yet in other things she had the advantage."[18]

Rachel fell head first into the "comparison trap" and the cost was hindrance to prayer. By looking at her sister and comparing herself to her, Rachel had once again placed something other than God in her view.

It's all too easy to focus on what we don't have, and forget what we do have. So easy to notice our handicaps that we miss our advantages. As a boy, I read about the life of George Washington Carver, who faced a series of challenges all his own. Yet one of his favorite poems written by Edgar A. Guest outlines a greater perspective on life's challenges and difficulties:

EQUIPMENT

Figure it out for yourself, my lad,
You've all that the greatest of men have had,
Two arms, two hands, two legs, two eyes
And a brain to use if you would be wise.

With this equipment they all began,
So start for the top and say, "I can."

Look them over, the wise and great
They take their food from a common plate,
And similar knives and forks they use,

---

[17] Henry, Matthew, and Leslie F. Church. Commentary on the whole Bible: Genesis to Revelation. Grand Rapids, MI: Zondervan Pub. House, 1961. Print.
[18] Henry, Matthew, and Leslie F. Church. Commentary on the whole Bible: Genesis to Revelation. Grand Rapids, MI: Zondervan Pub. House, 1961. Print.

With similar laces they tie their shoes.
The world considers them brave and smart,
But you've all they had when they made their start.

You can triumph and come to skill,
You can be great if you only will.
You're well equipped for what fight you choose,
You have legs and arms and a brain to use,
And the man who has risen great deeds to do
Began his life with no more than you.

You are the handicap you must face,
You are the one who must choose your place,
You must say where you want to go,
How much you will study the truth to know.
God has equipped you for life, but He
Lets you decide what you want to be.

Courage must come from the soul within,
The man must furnish the will to win.
So figure it out for yourself, my lad.
You were born with all that the great have had,
With your equipment they all began,
Get hold of yourself and say: "I can."

Paul reminded the Ephesians that "For we are His workmanship, created in Christ Jesus for good works, which God prepared beforehand so that we would walk in them." If we are God's workmanship, prepared beforehand, then being a copy of another is a suicide mission destined to fail. "God won't bless who you pretend to be," or try to be. God will only bless who he made you to be in Him.

Paul admonished the Corinthians saying that when they "measure themselves by themselves and compare themselves with themselves, they were without understanding." They lacked understanding because they lacked divine perspective. Comparison causes us to measure ourselves by another's estimation of us, rather than by the will of God for our own lives. In fact the greatest culprit is actually our own estimation of ourselves in comparison to others. The reality is that comparison is a great thief.

Theodor Roosevelt famously said that "comparison is the thief of joy," and he was right. The life which lives in the comparison trap never knows true joy because it is constantly eluded by someone else's achievements. Not only does comparison rob us of joy, but it also robs us of our God-given identity. Rachel was hands down the beloved of Jacob, fairer in beauty and more regarded. Yet her constant comparison with the other women led her to lose her identity in a quest to be what she thought others were.

If you live your life comparing your ministry to another, and your church to another, and your preaching to another, and your singing to another, before long you have lost your God-given identity and purpose in another. But most tragic of all, comparison robs our prayers of their power.

When our prayers are motivated by comparison they become selfish and ineffective. James tells us "You ask and do not receive, because you ask with wrong motives, so that you may spend it on your pleasures." It seems clear that Rachel's prayers were hindered in part due to succumbing to the comparison trap.

Furthermore there was the issue that "the Lord had withheld this from her."[19] It's one thing to pray for fruitfulness under an open heaven, and yet another to pray when the heavens are shut.

Have you ever prayed so earnestly for something that God seemed determined not to give it to you? How difficult it is to yield our will to the will of God, and accept his providence with contentment. Genesis 30:22 recounts the fact that "God remembered Rachel, and gave heed to her and opened her womb." What seemed like a divine "no" had only been a divine "wait!" And now the favored wife would give birth to a favored son.

A Boy Named Increase

Rachel named her first born son, Joseph which means "the

---

[19] Genesis 3:2

Lord has added to me." After having gone without a son for so long, Rachel named her son "adder" or "increase." Within the name is hidden a prayer for yet another son. Yet Joseph's name was prophetic in ways which Rachel most likely never understood. He would in fact be the source of increase for many. Herein we find in the giving of his name a striking parallel between Joseph and Christ.

The Bible scholar Arthur Pink wrote insightfully on this point:

"It is most significant that our patriarch had two names-Joseph, and Zaphnath-paaneah (Gen. 41:45) which translates "Revealer of secrets." This latter name was given to him by Pharaoh in acknowledgment of the Divine wisdom which was in him. Thus, Joseph may be said to be his human name and Zaphnath-paaneah, his Divine name. So, also, the one whom Joseph foreshadowed has a double name- "Jesus" being His human name, "Christ" signifying "the Anointed" of God, or, again, we have his double name in "Son of Man" which speaks of His humanity, and "Son of God" which tells of His Deity."[20]

Further Pink points out that "Joseph" means adding. The first Adam was the great subcontractor, the last Adam is the great Adder: through the one, men became lost; by the other, all who believe are saved. Christ is the One who "adds" to Heaven's inhabitants. Joseph was an adder just has the Christ he typified.

Joseph would add to people everywhere he went. In the tents of Jacob he brought an increase of joy and fulfilment. And as a slave in the house of Potiphar he brought an increase and blessing to his master. Genesis states that "It came about that from the time he made him overseer in his house and over all that he owned, the LORD blessed the Egyptian's house on account of Joseph; thus the LORD'S blessing was upon all that he owned, in the house and in the field."[21]

In the prison Joseph would add to the jailer by being a

---

[20] Pink, Arthur Walkington. Gleanings in Genesis. New York, NY: "Our hope", 1922. Print.
[21] Genesis 39:5

trustworthy and responsible inmate. Scripture records that "The chief jailer committed to Joseph's charge all the prisoners who were in the jail; so that whatever was done there, he was responsible for it. The chief jailer did not supervise anything under Joseph's charge because the LORD was with him; and whatever he did, the LORD made to prosper."[22] Then Joseph would add to the lives of his cellmates by interpreting the drams of the butler and the baker.

It may be difficult to imagine that in a series of life's cruel and intolerable reverses a man could think of adding to anyone else. Yet this was the life of the "adder." Eventually we will see him rise to the palace, and Joseph will add to the life of Pharaoh and eventually all of Egypt and the world. But the most remarkable twist in this saga is the fact that Joseph's story ends by adding to the lives of the very men who had sold him into slavery.

This ultimately is God's purpose for each of our lives that we would add to the lives of others. Not only were you meant to increase in fruitfulness but you were made to bring increase to the lives of others. John Maxwell has pointed out that a leader "adds value to people."[23] Value is anything you do to increase the ability of someone else to achieve their own dream. There is a great deception in the human condition; we are led to believe that each must get his own, and hold on tight once he has it. But the paradox of scripture presents another reality all together.

The bible teaches a reality in which those who "save their own life will lose it, but those who lose their life"[24] find it. The worldview of scripture teaches us that givers gain and keepers lose even what they have. "There is one who scatters, and yet increases all the more, and there is one who withholds what is justly due, and yet it results only in want."

The concept of being an adder is countercultural in our day,

---

[22] Genesis 39:22-23
[23] Maxwell, John C. The 21 irrefutable laws of leadership: follow them and people will follow you. Nashville, TN: Thomas Nelson Publishers, 1998, pg 47
[24] Matthew 16:25

yet it is the very path to being most like our maker. God is a giver, who adds value to our lives and desires that we be like Him. The book of Proverbs tell us that "The generous man will be prosperous, And he who waters will himself be watered." But let me translate that in another way "he who adds to others, will be added to."

Because I know humanity, I can say without fear of contradiction that there are people in your life who need to be watered. Like plants in need of the life giving properties of H^2O, there are people in our life who need the water which we have.

In the first regard there are people who need the "water of the Word." They need to hear the Gospel, because "like cold water to a weary soul, so is good news from a distant land."

Others may need an encouraging word in season to water the anxiety of their soul. With this comes a great promise that those who water will themselves be watered. This is the pattern established by God.

God gave a son and received multitudes of sons in return. When we add to others, God sees to it that we are added to in return. This is the age old principle of sowing and reaping. When you sow into the lives of others, you reap from many sources. "No one has ever become poor by giving."[25]

In a sermon in the Metropolitan Tabernacle Charles Spurgeon said:

"The general principle is that in living for the good of others, we shall be profited ourselves. We must not isolate our own interests, but feel that we live for others. This teaching is sustained by the analogy of nature, for in nature there is a law that no one thing can be independent of the rest of creation, but there is a mutual action and reaction of all upon all. All the constituent parts of the universe are bound to one another by invisible chains, and there is not a single creature in it which springs up, or

---

[25] Frank, Anne. Anne Frank: the diary of a young girl. New York: Bantam , 1993. Print.

flourishes, or decays itself alone. The very planets, though they float far from one another, exercise attraction; and the fixed stars, though they seem to be infinitely remote, are still linked to one another by mysterious bonds. God has so constituted this universe that selfishness is the greatest possible offense against His law, and living for others, and ministering to others is the strictest obedience to His will."[26]

The value of adding value to others is immeasurable, especially in the fruit it bears in our own lives. This is true because bringing increase to others is obedience to the will of God, and God honors those who honor him. In my own life I can point to the very moments when value has been added to me.

I can still recall my fifth grade class at Pettus Elementary with the indomitable Mrs. Bell. Her life motto was "oh well." It seemed nothing could get her down, anytime someone messed up she would say "oh well." Of course I hated that motto, being a fifth grader I wanted petty things to matter, yet disappointments didn't seem to matter much to her. I was not the best student academically, in spite of my love for books. I had developed into a slow reader, and my spelling was notably atrocious.

One day Mrs. Bell called me over to her desk and said, "Isaac, I'm going to give you these two books." She handed me a dictionary and a thesaurus, and said, "You will need these, because God has given you the gift of words."

"Oh Well Mrs. Bell" as I came to know her, did not know that day how much value she added to my life. The fact that she had looked past my deficiency and had seen my potential was a defining moment in my young life. From that moment on I knew that whatever I lacked in my own knowledge could be made up for in the study of those two books, and to this day I live by the principle that I'm not defined by what I lack if I was willing to seek the answer.

We have all known generous people, and if you're like me you

---

[26] "The Waterer Watered -- C. H. Spurgeon.". N.p., n.d. Web. 17 Jan. 2017.

have desired to live generously. There is something attractive about generosity, which inspires the human heart. In my own life I have known generous people, one of whom was my paternal grandfather. Every memory I have of Ruben De Los Santos includes him with his hand extended in giving. Whether it was an itinerant preacher, or a passing friend, my Grandfather could be counted on for a generous gift.

As I recall his home, in which I spent much time as a child, I know that he and my grandmother never enjoyed a single luxury. They didn't have air-conditioning, or even a television. They weren't poor, but the simplicity of their home would not have told you as much. Yet it seems to me in retrospect that those luxuries which they may have enjoyed were sown as gifts into the lives of others. In so doing, they shared in the soul winning ministry of countless preachers, four of their own sons and two grandsons became Pastors.

Being an adder who brings increase to others is a calling which each of us must embrace. It is the death nail to pride and self-seeking, and sets us up for fulfillment. How we add value to others may take many different shapes and forms, but it is the "surest road to our own happiness to seek the good of our fellows."[27] Does your life add to the lives of others?

---

[27] "The Waterer Watered -- C. H. Spurgeon." N.p., n.d. Web. 17 Jan. 2017.

Chapter Two

The Coat

"Joseph, when seventeen years of age, was pasturing the flock with his brothers while he was still a youth, along with the sons of Bilhah and the sons of Zilpah, his father's wives. And Joseph brought back a bad report about them to their father. Now Israel loved Joseph more than all his sons, because he was the son of his old age; and he made him a varicolored tunic." Genesis 37:2-3

The tents of Jacob were filled with the sound of a newborn, and all the attention was on Joseph. Rachel and Jacob were doting parents without apology, and their love of Joseph made their love of all others look like hate. Scriptures tells us that Jacob "fashioned and bestowed" upon Joseph a coat of many colors. The terms in the original imply the precise and careful design of garment made for Joseph alone. The terms used in the Hebrew language would best describe a coat of royalty or nobility. This garment was the unique expression of the father's favor upon his son, and also a sign of the father's blessing on his son. While from the perspective of his other sons, Jacobs gift was over the top, and ostentatious, to Joseph this gift would mark his life with purpose.

Through careful planning Jacob must have designed a coat that would have cost a small fortune. Jacob must have taken great pains in preparing this gift for Joseph, and in doing so he reveals to us the heart of God.

The fact is that our heavenly father has fashioned and

bestowed on us a coat which fits only us. Our lives are filled with gifts and purpose painstakingly designed by our Father to accomplish his divine agenda. We all have a coat which our Father has given us, and which we must wear in order to accomplish our God-given purpose. Considering the attention it would draw, and the vehemence it would evoke from Joseph's brothers, one might think it better to hide the coat in a closet. But Joseph would wear his coat with great zeal, and even after it was taken from him he would wear the spiritual mantle till his dying day.

Dreams Released

Not until Jacob gave Joseph the coat of many colors does the Scripture record that Joseph dreamt any dreams. Yet once the coat had been given to Joseph a shift took place in his life, and I dare say in his spirit. A spiritual impartation had taken place which opened to Joseph the path of destiny, and exposed him to the gift of God. A casual reading of the Joseph story would lead one to believe that Joseph dreamt dreams which sprung from a prideful boy's ambition. Yet a careful reading of the same would reveal that Joseph's dreams were prophetic in nature and revealed not only his divine purpose but also the destiny of the nation of Israel. These dreams did not come, nor were they released into his life until he had his father's blessing through the impartation of the mantle.

We see here a pattern which would be repeated through scripture on multiple occasions, the pattern of impartation from spiritual fathers to spiritual sons. There is a great lesson to be learned in the relationship between the giving of the coat and the release of dreams into Joseph's life. The blessing of a father has a unique and divinely inspired ability to shape the destiny of a son. A father's voice can build steel into a sons resolve, or gelatin in place of bones depending on his choice. We will examine that pattern in the lives of Joshua, Elisha, Saul of Tarsus, and Timothy.

Moses and Joshua

Perhaps the greatest example of this pattern of impartation in terms of its scale is the succession of Moses by Joshua. The coat Joshua would wear in the book that bears his name must have fallen upon him like a lead cloak. For he would fill the shoes of no less than the greatest prophet in Jewish history, and that would be no small feat. Yet thanks for Moses impartation of responsibility and character into his life, Joshua would actually do more than Moses had accomplished before him.

Responsibility before Promotion

We first see in this relationship that Moses gave Joshua the weight of true responsibility. Joshua demonstrated a great degree of responsibility in taking on the command of the army in the Battle against Amalek. The command of a citizen army, armed no better than runaway slaves was no small challenge. Yet when instructed by Moses to choose men and go out and fight Amalek, he uttered no word questioning the order. Moses demonstrated as a spiritual father the willingness to let the mantle fall upon his protégé and trust God with the outcome.

Joshua distinguished himself by being a courageous leader, whose victory secured Israel's peace. His victory there was singled out by the Lord who said to Moses in the aftermath "Write this on a scroll as something to be remembered and <u>make sure that Joshua hears it</u>, because I will completely blot out the name of Amalek from under heaven."[28] From this we ought to note that responsibility comes before promotion. No one ever deserves the place of a protégé simply because they are related to the leader. In fact few of the great biblical successions were nepotistic, and those that were failed historically as in the case of the sons of Gideon, Samuel, and even David. Perhaps this is because they leaned too heavily on the biological relationship to the man, never gaining the spirit of the man.

Responsibility helps a protégé learn the heart of his leader, and the more responsibility he can handle, the closer he comes to being worthy of the mantle. Each battle you help your leader win, will plant the seeds for the battles you will win when you are in command. Joshua's record for military conquest is paralleled by none in Scripture. And all of those battles were the fruit of Joshua's service to Moses, the Servant of the Lord.

---

[28] Exodus 17:14

Humility before Honor

In Numbers 11 we get another glimpse at the relationship between these two men. At this point in the wilderness journey the Lord instructed Moses to empower 70 elders of Israel with his spirit. As a result of this impartation the elders began to prophecy through the camp of Israel with great affect.

As word of this reached Joshua, he became jealous for Moses. He said "Moses, my lord, restrain them."[29] Moses asked "Are you jealous for my sake? Would that all the Lord's people were prophets, and that the Lord would put His spirit upon them."[30]

Two things we should draw from this episode. First that humility comes before honor. For Moses the desire for self-preservation was subordinate to the good of the Nation. Every true leader loves to have his people engaging in the gifts and callings of God. It is a small man who cannot rejoice in the success of those under his charge. He taught Joshua that other people's gifts do not diminish our own. If you ever have to smear others so that you can glow, you are a weak leader.

Secondly, we find an endearing quality in Joshua's jealously for Moses. He was jealous for the man of God, ready to defend his place of honor against any intruder. What a remarkable quality. He teaches us to honor our leaders, and to defend them against those who would abuse their office. So often a protégé may be tempted divulge the details gained in confidence. Or perhaps to judge harshly the failing of the man he's been called to serve.

Being near enough to someone to profit from their example also means you are close enough to observe their faults. In that place of confidence you must be careful to honor that intimacy with safety. This of course does not mean we cover sin, but we do defend those whom we have been called to serve. When temped to use your proximity against your leader, choose honor instead. Choose rather to defend the place of nearness you have been given and defend them with love. This too is the seed of your future.

---

[29] Numbers 11:28
[30] Numbers 11:29

Stick to God like Glue

Another phrase that captures my thoughts is in Exodus 33:11. Moses is communing with God in the tent of meeting. This moment was crucial for Israel and the tension was palpable throughout the camp of Israel. The Lord had told Moses that he will not continue with Israel on their Journey toward the promise land. They have grieved the Lord, and Moses stands in the place of intersession for them.

The Word states that the Lord met face to face with Moses, and Joshua "would not depart from the tent."[31] Joshua knew that this was a critical moment for Moses and for Israel, and he determined to be present to serve Moses and hear from God. Joshua stuck to God and Moses like glue.

This lesson must not be lost on the modern protégé, because leadership is about more than public recognition. There is a vital element in spiritual leadership that demands a private relationship with God. It demands an altar of prayerful communion with God. From this secret life comes public power.

It also involves faithfulness in the shadows, and commitment in the place of obscurity. It's easy to serve in public, where crowds celebrate your service. But it's a different thing all together to serve in the shadow of a man like Moses, for 40 years. Joshua seems to have done this with a smile on his face, and a outstanding contentment with his office.

The Witness of Moses

After forty years of faithful service to Moses, Joshua was commissioned to assume the leadership of Israel. The Mentor-Protégé relationship had run its course and now it was time to pass the baton. The scriptures state that "Moses called Joshua...in the presence of all of Israel"[32] and spoke the words which would release Joshua into the Ministry of Conquest. He told Israel "Joshua is the one who will cross ahead of you"[33] making it clear

---

[31] Exodus 33:11
[32] Deuteronomy 31:7

that it was Joshua who was to lead. The witness of Moses was clear and emphatic, thus removing the confusion of unplanned transition. Having experienced a couple of transitions in my life, I know how crucial this witness was.

First of all, the witness of Moses was important to Joshua. For Joshua the burden of this responsibility was going to be great, and knowing that Moses had endorsed him would be a vital source of encouragement in days of trouble. If you are a "Moses" in someone's life, please keep this in mind. Your words and witness over the life of your successor are tremendously important and powerful.

Many "Joshuas" today crave the words of their "Moses," and do not have them. "All successors crave the approval and encouragement only a predecessor can offer."[34]   Moses' words were no less than inspiring when you consider the scale of their importance.   This was not a Pastor telling the new guy you will lead this church to a new building program. This was not a CEO saying "You will achieve greater gains for the company after I'm gone." Joshua would give Israel possession of an entire country.

Moses declared, "Be strong and courageous, for you shall go with this people into the land which the LORD has sworn to their fathers to give them, and you shall give it to them as an inheritance. The LORD is the one who goes ahead of you; He will be with you. He will not fail you or forsake you. Do not fear or be dismayed."[35]   Surely no day would pass in Joshua's ministry, in which he would not recall the words of Moses.

Secondly, the witness of Moses was important for the people of Israel. They also needed to know that a man had been prepared for them. And when the time came for transition, the people were ready to follow the man with the coat which Moses had given him.

---

[33] Deuteronomy 31:3
[34] Mullins, Tom. Passing the Leadership Baton. Thomas Nelson, Nashville TN. 2015 Pg 37
[35] Deuteronomy 31:7-8

Elijah and Elisha

If Moses and Joshua are the best example in terms of scale, then Elijah and Elisha are the greatest example in terms of the anointing being imparted. Elijah was known and revered for his prophetic exploits. His life had marked Israel in a powerful way. And now came a time for his departure. Led by God as to who his replacement would be, Elijah descended Mount Horeb where he had been praying for forty days on a mission to anoint two kings and a successor.

Meanwhile in a field far way, there was the diligent Elisha plowing without a thought as to what was about to happen to him. He was by all accounts, an ordinary man, just an average Joe. He was working man and a godly man to boot.

A few times while flying from one city to another, I have heard the pilot say "Ladies and gentleman, we have arrived at our destination, but we are in a holding pattern right now." A holding pattern is "the flight path maintained by an aircraft awaiting permission to land."

Sometimes when you are in a holding pattern, you fly around in a big rectangle, until the tower gives the pilot permission to land. Elisha was in just such a spot. Not going anywhere, but being very faithful with the work he had anyway.

This is an important principle to learn, because we must be willing to work while we wait. In fact everyone who Jesus called to be his disciple was working when he called them. God loves to call on working men and women; we are faithful in the holding pattern. God often uses holding patterns in our live to prepare us for the next level. And if we are faithful with this season, He will give us the next.

God Is Talking To Someone About You

I believe there are three witnesses to every call. When God calls someone he first speaks to them; that's the first witness. Then He speaks to those in spiritual authority about them; that's the second witness. Then he speaks to everyone about them; that's the third witness. I suspect that Elisha knew that he was created for more. Without a doubt God had spoken to him about himself and had placed a since of purpose in his heart.

Yet when we first see Elisha we don't see a man jockeying for position, or networking with movers and shakers. We see him minding his own business and positioned for an encounter with divine purpose. He had his daily routine down to a science, and nothing about his life may have seemed destined for greatness. But God knew where he was, and while Elisha was ploughing God was talking to Elijah about him and there was the second witness.

Maybe you are in a holding pattern right now in your own life. Maybe you are wondering when your day will come. Can I encourage you to be faithful in the work you have before you right now. Perhaps while you read this book, God is talking to someone about you.

When I was five-years old my Pastor announced that an evangelist was coming to our church the following Saturday evening. We lived next door to the church, and I can recall with vivid detail my anticipation about his arrival. David Garcia was a man in his seventies, and had nothing in common with a five-year-old boy to be sure. I had no reason to be excited about his coming, but something within me made me anxious for his visit. All day long I waited, running to the window to see if he had arrived. I kept asking my mother throughout the day, "Is he here yet?" Then again "Mom, when is he coming?" She finally said "Isaac, what is the deal with David Garcia, he will be here when he gets here!"

At long last the evening came; we dressed for the service and walked over to the church. I sat up front as if expecting a grand prize, though I really had no reason for this great expectation. The service began and the preacher was nowhere to be found. He as late, and I was beginning to worry that he would not arrive at all.

Finally, the man of God walked through the door of that old country church. He came straight up to the pulpit to begin his message. He asked the congregation to open their bibles to a given passage, and then he paused. "Who are the parents of this little boy," he asked. My parents signaled who they were from the back row, and he began to prophecy. He said, "This child has been called by God to preach His Word, and he will go to the nations.

He will be great among the great and small among the small."

It still amazes me to think that even at five-years old, God was talking to someone about me. With those words the old Prophet became the second witness to the call of God on my life.

Pouring Water on Elijah's Hands

Thus it was for Elisha, that "while he was plowing with twelve pairs of oxen before him, and he with the twelfth. And Elijah passed over to him and threw his mantle on him."[36] Elisha, obviously aware that this was his moment of purpose immediately "left the oxen and ran after Elijah ... and ministered to him."[37] So began the ministry of Elisha. In fact the scriptures sum up the ministry of Elisha to Elijah by saying that he was the one "who used to pour water on the hands of Elijah."[38] Literally Elisha was the servant called upon to pour water upon Elijah's hands. That hardly seems like a step up from plowing, but in that place of service a spiritual mantle was being passed.

In the first place it offered Elisha an up close and personal look into the private life of the prophet of God. Elisha would get to know more than Elijah's public face, he would get to know the man as he truly was.

Secondly, this would offer Elisha a lesson in faithfulness over the stewardship of small responsibilities. Jesus said "And if you have not been faithful in the use of that which is another's, who will give you that which is your own?"[39]

Finally, pouring water on Elijah's hands was a glimpse into the spiritual life of Elijah. According to Jewish custom, one could not enter into prayer without washing their hands. Thus Elisha would have an up-close look at the prayer life of his mentor.

If you can learn anything from those in spiritual leadership

---

[36] 1 Kings 19:19
[37] 1 Kings 19:19-21
[38] 2 Kings 3:11
[39] Luke 16:12

over you, seek to learn to pray as they do. Even Jesus' disciples asked him "Master, teach us to pray."[40]

In my own life, I have coveted more than anything the moments which I have spent eavesdropping on my father's prayers. I can recall as a boy hearing my father pray, and as a young man being invited to fast with him for three days shut in with God. I have also enjoyed many occasions to spend time in prayer beside another Spiritual Father, Dr. Jimmy Longoria the Bishop of the Unified Pentecostal Local Churches. I've lost more than a few half hours of prayer overhearing his prayers and making them my own. I'm always amazed at the power and precision of his prayers. I've listened with intent as he called out name after name in solemn petition before the living God.

Further still, I treasure moments I've spent with Pastor Samuel Montoya of Sinai Pentecostal Church, who has been a mentor to me. His prayers seem to flow quietly from an inexpressibly tender heart. Often through tears I have heard him utter prayers, and even some on my behalf. Those moments listening to my fathers pray have marked my life forever and have taught me more about the Christian life than ten thousand sermons ever could. Truly we must say "Teach us to pray."

We see the mantle placed upon Elisha at the beginning of his ministry, and we witness it fall upon him after the translation of Elijah into heaven. But it was the nearness to Elijah that prepared Elisha to carry it.

Barnabas and Saul

Now there were at Antioch, in the church that was there, prophets and teachers: Barnabas, and Simeon who was called Niger, and Lucius of Cyrene, and Manaen who had been brought up with Herod the tetrarch, and Saul. While they were ministering to the Lord and fasting, the Holy Spirit said, "Set apart for Me Barnabas and Saul for the work to which I have called them. Then, when they had fasted and prayed and laid their hands on them, they sent them away."

[40] Luke 11:1

32

We see the pattern again in Acts 13, when the elders of the church at Antioch were praying. As they prayed the Holy Spirit moved upon the elders and told them to "Set apart for Me Barnabas and Saul for the work to which I have called them."

The elders "laid hands on them and sent them away." This impartation gave birth to the first missionary journey in Church history, and would lead to the planting of Churches in Asia Minor. It is my conviction that the elements in this passage reveal the principles which must be practiced by the 21st Century Church if it hopes to see 1st Century results.

First, we see the inescapable role of prayer in the release of divine insight and strategy. No believer should ever hope to accomplish great things for God, receive strategies which will impact nations, or change generations without fervent and effectual prayer. To the degree that the church has delayed in seeing the manifestation of Kingdom power in our day, we must lay the fault at the feet of prayerlessness within our ranks.

I have read the better part of the church growth books written in the last five years, and am dismayed to find an incredible lack of advice concerning the need to pray through, for divine strategy. It is my guess that most writers take for granted that their readers will employ the weapon of prayer. Yet In the balance of those books there seems to be a greater reliance on the power of manmade ideas which might work, as compared to the release of divine direction which cannot fail.

Secondly, we should note the repeated pattern of impartation on the part of the elders. In this case we see specifically the laying on of hands, this ancient ritual seemingly only symbolic bears the marks of divine origin, and holds the key to many blessings. Paul would write to his own son[41] in the faith, saying to Timothy, "Do not neglect the spiritual gift within you, which was bestowed on you through prophetic utterance with the laying on of hands by the presbytery."[42] Some struggle with the idea that simply laying hands upon someone could impart gifts, and yet this is precisely

---

[41] 1 Timothy 1:2
[42] 1 Timothy 4:14

33

what Paul is saying.

I have witnessed with my own eyes the power of this sacred act of impartation, and bear witness to its validity. In 2005 I attended my denomination's national convention, and was before the presbytery which recognizes ministers for the ministry. I will never forget the moment when they called me in and stated that they had recognized my calling and extended to me the license to preach.

To my surprise the three men, spiritual fathers and mentors, asked me to kneel and after anointing me with oil they laid their hands upon me and commissioned me for wider ministry. That moment was sacred and life changing, as I walked under the assurance that God called me, and that He had made that calling clear to others as well. I always knew that I had been called, and the fruit of my ministry thus far had born witness to that call. Yet even Jesus had public testimony of his calling, and through the laying on of hands by presbytery we too have public witness of an inner call.

Now I have had the privilege of serving on that presbytery and have been witness to many prayers of ordination, wherein I have seen the noted impact of the ministry of impartation. Some due to denominational reluctance downplay the value of such an act, but my study of scripture and testimony of my experience can only rise in calling the church back to the spirit empowered ministry of impartation.

The Power of The Spoken Blessing

Yet the laying on of hands is not the only form which impartation takes. Another form is the spoken word. Paul told Timothy that the gifts were imparted to him through the *"prophetic utterance."* You recognize this practice in the old testament teaching of the "Blessing." The blessing was a verbal pronouncement of Gods intention over a person or a people. We see that the first wedding boasted of a "blessing from YHWH."[43] Genesis 50 is full of the prophetically significant blessings of Jacob

---

[43] Genesis 5:2

upon his sons. In Numbers 6, the Lord's commands the priest of Israel to Bless the people saying: The Lord bless you and keep you; The Lord make His face shine upon you, And be gracious to you; The Lord lift up His countenance upon you, And give you peace.

In my own Pastorate, I have adopted the practice of blessing the people each week, and have seen God fulfill His word over them in remarkable ways. I have seen countless times how words spoken in blessing over this precious flock that I have the honor of serving, have been fulfilled to the letter. I personally believe that praying prophetic blessings or engaging in the ministry of impartation as such is not the speaker causing heaven to move to its will, but rather speaking what heaven has revealed to be the will of God.

The spoken word has long been recognized as powerful, and yet in this context, silence may even be fatal. I am convinced that many gifts lie dormant in the body of Christ today, because the "prophetic word" or "blessing" has been silenced or undervalued. And the ministry of impartation had not been practiced.

Paul and Timothy

Perhaps one of the most raw stories of this Father and Son relationship occurs in the New Testament book of Acts. Here we find the venerable Apostle Paul has taken under his wing the young and gifted Timothy. I have been fascinated by this account since I was in college. My professor made a statement which has directed my relationship choices along the way. He said "every man needs three men in his life; a Paul, a Barnabas, and Timothy." We all need a Paul to teach us, a Barnabas to walk beside us, and Timothy to train after us. Timothy was certainly a man who Paul trained and entrusted with great responsibility.

Timothy was from the city of Lystra in Asia Minor, and was no doubt a witness to Paul's ministry in that city. It was at Lystra that Paul was stoned by a mob and left for dead, only to get up and continue his ministry. Here he had demonstrated not with words but with deeds the great commitment which was required by those who would be followers of Christ. Among these witnesses to his ministry there was this young man named Timothy. He was raised in Jewish religion by his mother, but he was uncircumcised as a result of having a Greek father.

The bible calls him a "disciple...well-spoken of by the brethren."[44] He was obviously well regarded and trusted by Paul. Timothy would come alongside the Apostle to serve him and often was sent as a representative to the churches. So significant was Paul's investment in this man, the two of the New Testament epistles are written to him. First and Second Timothy contain the treasure trove of Pastoral Theology which we are mining to his day.

Circumcising A Son

While a detailed discussion of the Paul–Timothy relationship is outside the scope of this volume, I would like to focus on one episode which I believe says it all. It's a peculiar portion of scripture which leaves many of us puzzled. But upon embarking on the second leg of his second missionary journey Paul chose to take Timothy along. However the place that they were going was well populated by Jews, and Paul understood that Timothy would have problems gaining acceptance due to his Greek linage.

So we read that "Paul wanted this man to go with him; and he took him and circumcised him because of the Jews who were in those parts, for they all knew that his father was a Greek."[45] I mentioned that this leaves many puzzled because in Galatians chapter two Paul forbade Titus to be circumcised on account of the fact the salvation was not through circumcision but rather grace. Yet the two incidents do have different and distinct reasons.

In Titus's case, Paul was defending the gospel against judaizers who sought to enslave Greeks through the practice of the Mosaic law. In Timothy's case, Paul seems to be preparing Timothy for ministry among the Jews. Paul apparently realized that in order for Timothy to be given an ear from a Jewish audience, he must comply with the custom.

---

[44] Acts 16:3
[45] Acts 16:3

What we see here is that Paul was willing to do what all spiritual fathers must do. He was willing to circumcise his son. In the scriptures the physical act of circumcision represented the cutting away of the impurity of the flesh.   It represented separation from the carnal nature. Thus Paul demonstrates that a father must be willing to circumcise his son, to correct his path in such a way as to make him effective. This same act was carried out by Abraham to Isaac, and by Jacob over his sons.

In fact, God nearly killed Moses on the road to Egypt, for refusing to circumcise his sons. For Paul the imparting his mantle to Timothy, included the removal of hindrances to the purpose of God in Timothy's life.   In his case it was the physical act of circumcision, but for us today we could call it good old-fashion discipline.

The great tragedy of the fatherless generation which America has today, is the loss of discipline and correction among our youth. Undisciplined boys become undisciplined men; and such men wreak havoc on society. In a world where everyone does what is right in their own eyes, there is increasing blindness. This failure to discipline must not be so in the world of Spiritual Fathers and Sons. Spiritual mantles are not merely the passing on of good things, but also the cutting away of evil things.

Can You Stand To Be Corrected

We still need prophets like Nathan who will stand in our face and say "you are that man"[46] as he pointed out the guilt in David. That cutting rebuke of Israel's King, saved his reign. We need men like Paul who "withstood" Peter to his face" because he was clearly condemned."[47] Sons need their fathers to call things like they see them, and challenge the deviations they take from the path. These moments of correction never feel good, often they leave us reeling. But I assure you that when those corrections come from a "father," who has invested into us they always bring a benefit to the soul. And therein lays a great truth.

---

[46] 2 Samuel 12:17
[47] Galatians 2:11

Relationship alone gives one the right to cut and rebuke. You can never effectively correct a man with whom you have no relationship. Fathers alone could present their sons for circumcision. No one in all of the first century church could have prompted a grown man like Timothy to be circumcised. No one, not even his own biological father had not done so. No one that is, but Paul. The man whose investment of relationship into Timothy had forged a bond of faith and trust.

There is such power in a father's voice, especially in his ability to call out of his child gifts which the child himself may not see. As in the cases I have mentioned above, each father spoke destiny into the life of their son, and that son rose to meet it by God's grace.

It cannot be to simply stated that impartation through the laying on of Hands, at the leading of the Holy Spirit, by spiritual fathers, to spiritual sons is the Old and New Testament pattern by which destiny is released. Any church that hopes to enjoy the release of divine purpose, must embrace Gods pattern and practice it.

Chapter Three

Does
The Church
Have No Sons

Thus says the LORD: "Does Israel have no sons? Or has he no heirs? Why then has Malcam taken possession of Gad And his people settled in its cities? "Therefore behold, the days are coming," declares the LORD, "That I will cause a trumpet blast of war to be heard Against Rabbah of the sons of Ammon; And it will become a desolate heap, And her towns will be set on fire. Then Israel will take possession of his possessors." Jeremiah 49:1-2

The words of the Prophet Jeremiah were sent ringing in my ears. "Does Israel have no sons, or has he no heirs." I had been praying about the apparent apathy among my generation and those that are failing to pursue the ministry as a vocation. It seemed to me that there was a growing gap between those who abandoned all to preach and those who saw preaching has a hobby for active Christians until a career came along. As I prayed the Lord spoke from His word. Jeremiah 49:1 "Does Israel have no sons, or has he no heirs." Except, as I read it I heard in my sprit "Does the church have no sons?"

Could it be that God gave two thousand years of church history sons like Luther, Wesley, Spurgeon, or Whitfield, but had now left the church without sons? Of course this was not the case. Then where are these sons? Where are the heirs of Christian Ministry? I believe that the Sons of the Church are waiting for Fathers to release them into their ministry. They are waiting for an Elijah to throw his mantle over them. I believe that the sons of the church are crying out for Spiritual Fathers. I believe that spiritual fathers have neglected their role of raising up sons. Further, I believe that the sons of the church have no idea what it means to be a son.

In this chapter, I will set before you the fact that Spiritual Sonship is the apex of Christian Doctrine, and furthermore lay out for us the fact that Sonship is the pattern for releasing Gods purpose and ministry.

Sonship—The Apex of Christian Doctrine

Have you ever asked yourself "What does it mean to be a son?" If you are like me, the question of what goes into being a son probably never crossed your mind. The fact is that for the most part we see Sonship as a passive reality, which we had nothing to do with. Most of us think of being a son or daughter as the product of other people's actions, namely our parents, and not as an aim or goal to be obtained.

In contrast, when a man becomes a father he usually spends at least some time meditating on the question of what it means to be a father. And if I ask you that question you would no doubt list things like progenitor, provider, and protector among others. It's obvious to us what a father is, and the fact is that fatherhood is not the result of passivity, but rather initiative, commitment, and effort.

Yet my question is not "What does it mean to be a father?" My question to you is "What does it mean to be a son?" I believe that we will discover together that true Sonship is not the result of passivity either but rather the result of conscious faith, which requires commitment and effort on our part.

The Doctrine of Sonship is the apex of bible doctrine. It is the aim of scripture as it unfolds to reveal to man his adoption into Gods family, through God's Son, by God's Spirit. To the extent that one understands this doctrine, one will enjoy the fullness of God the Father and all that Christ died to secure. J.I. Packer writes "For everything that Christ taught, everything that makes the New Testament new, and better than the Old, everything that is distinctively Christian as opposed to merely Jewish, is summed up in the knowledge of the Fatherhood of God. "Father' is the Christian name of God. Our understanding of Christianity cannot be better than our grasp of adoption."[48] Sadly many Christians live as orphans rather than sons, not because they do not have a heavenly Father, but because they have not come to know Him.

Relationship with the Father is the high water mark of Christian experience. Jesus said "I am the way, the truth, and the life. And no one comes God to the Father except through me".[49] Derek Prince has stated that this verse speaks of "a pathway and a destination. Jesus is the pathway, the Father is the destination."[50] Jesus came to make a way to the Father. He came to introduce us to the Father, and to provide the means for our adoption into the Family of God.

This was necessary because contrary to the teaching of some, because God is not Father universally to all men. The gift of God as Father is received only through faith in His Son Jesus Christ. As J.I. Packer writes, "The gift of sonship to God becomes ours not through being born, but through being born again."[51] Yet once born again through the working of Grace in our hearts, the gift of sonship to God is completely ours.

Paul wrote the Galatian believers that in the "Fullness of time, God sent forth His son, born of a woman, born under Law, in order

---

[48] Packer, J.I. Knowing God. 1973 by J.I. Packer. InterVarsity Press. Downers Grove, IL. pp. 200-201.

[49] John 14:6

[50] "To Please My Father." Teaching Letter No. 17. Derek Prince http://www.derekprince.org/Articles/1000086997/DPM_USA/Arc hive_of_UK/Resources/Daily_Devotional/Resources/Jun_16.aspx

[51] Packer, J.I. Knowing God. 1973 by J.I. Packer. InterVarsity Press. Downers Grove, IL. pp. 200-201.

the He might redeem those who were under the Law, that we might receive the adoption as sons."[52] Plainly we see then that the Father sent Jesus with the every objective of adopting us as sons. Adoption is not merely a byproduct of Christ's coming, but the very motivation for it.

Then he adds the emphatic "And because you are son, God has sent forth the spirit of His son into our hearts, crying "Abba Father."[53] He states "You are sons." This is the gracious result of the new birth, and what a tremendous reality it is. It means we are no longer slaves to sin and fear. We are no longer orphans. We are "sons." John wrote in his prolog "That as many as received Him (Christ) to them He gave the right to become children of God."[54]

Now you may have noticed the absence of the word daughter in this context. That is simply because in the days of Paul the word daughter actually carried the implication of lesser rights. A daughter could not inherit property; hence all twelve tribes are sons. Yet the reality set forth by the apostle is that God has no daughters, he has no children with lesser rights. He only has sons. Male and female believers are given the rights of "sons."

As a seal of our adoption, God has given us "the Spirit of His Son," by which we call God Father. The believer can call God "Abba" or daddy, because he has the inner witness of having been adopted into His family. Jesus taught us to pray "Our Father, who is in heaven." Not our CEO who is in heaven. Not our Master who is in heaven. Not even our Maker who is in heaven. All of which are true but distant expressions of relationship. Rather he taught us to call God "Father," the nearest and precious expression of our new found relationship with God. So long as we see God as CEO, Boss, Maker, or even Master, but not as Father, we live outside of the privilege which God intended for us.

---

[52] Galatians 4:4-6
[53] Galatians 4:4-6
[54] John 1:12

Chosen

Note if you will, a few implications of this truth. First of all, being adopted means being chosen. The adoptee is the choice of the adopter. This is not accidental relationship. God has set his intention upon adopting you. Jesus said "You did not choose me, but I have chosen you." If you chose him, you could decide to leave Him. But friend, you did not choose Him, He chose you. He chose you and will not let you go. The next time you are tempted to feel like a spiritual orphan. Feeling like you are unworthy of God's Love. Feeling unworthy of Gods mercy or blessing. Just remember that he chose you. And he chose you knowing everything about you. "For He predestine us to adoption as sons through Jesus Christ to Himself, according to the kind intention of His will."[55]

A New Identity

Now note three immediate results of this adoption. The passage states that "You are no longer slaves, but a son; and if a son, then an heir through the gracious act of God." The first result of this adoption is a new identity, the identity of a son. Previously you were a slave, bearing the identity of sins bondage and shame. Now in Christ you have been given a new name, a new home address, and a new eternal destination.

Paul told the Corinthians "Who also sealed us and gave us the Spirit in our hearts as a pledge."[56] It literally means that God has set his seal of ownership upon us, making it plain that we are His. Having this identity means we no longer strive to be accepted by men, because we know that we are fully accepted in Christ.

In psychology they write about the hierarchy of needs. Third on the list of needs after food and shelter is the need to belong. This need to belong drives many to act out in unhealthy ways, adopting harmful practices for their lives. Yet when we are adopted into the family of God, we receive "sonship" which satisfies the hunger to belong.

---

[55] Ephesians 1:5
[56] 2 Corinthians 1:22

One indicator as to a person's sense of identity, comes through their use of the word "I." Statements like "I can't, I'm not valuable, or I'm stupid" reveal a person's internal sense of worth and identity. For this reason when you are part of the family of God, it is important to use words that remind you of your identity in Christ. You must dwell constantly in our new identity saying "I am a child of God."

A New Nature

Not only does adoption imply a new identity, but it also implies a new nature. For the passage states that God has " sent forth the spirit of His son into our hearts."[57] As a result of this spiritual adoption, the believers is now indwelt by the Holy Spirit of God. This means that the believer now has the nature of God, dwelling within. This and this alone facilitates the change and conversion of the believers. The fact that the power of God now dwells within enables the believer to live life in the Spirit. Therefore "put on the new self, which in the likeness of God has been created in righteousness and holiness of the truth."[58] When a child is adopted the new parents take him home, and give him all that they can to help him assimilate into the new family. However, the one thing they cannot give the child is their DNA. They cannot impart their genetic makeup, or composition. Yet spiritual adoption is not limited by this physical reality. When you are adopted into the family of God, God gives you the spiritual equivalent of His DNA, the Holy Spirit of God. Now you are indwelt by a new nature and have become a new man.

The bible elaborated on this idea with a comparison between the "old man" and the "new man." The old man is you without the nature of God. The new man is the person you become because you have been indwelt by God. The "old man" thinks little of lying, but "new man" puts away lying, and in its place speaks truth. The "old man" gets angry and lets it remain unchecked. The "new man" may get angry, but does not let the sun go down on your anger. The "old man" is willing to steal, but the "new man" stops stealing, choosing rather to work so that he can help someone in

---

[57] Galatians 4:4-6
[58] Ephesians 4:24

need. The "old man" has no thought for what comes out of his mouth. But a "new man" avoids "corrupt communication," seeking to say that which is elevating and inspiring to those who hear.

This new nature is like a new set of clothes. Clothes that the believer must choose to wear. This new spiritual garb is worn by faith in the one who wears it and must be put on by faith. Dr. John MacArthur states in his sermon on the New Man that "In the spiritual sense you need to dress yourself spiritually to meet your identity spiritually. That's his point right here. It's pretty simple. If you're a Christian, you ought to dress the part. A new man should wear new clothes. It's not talking about a Christian uniform. It's not talking about a certain kind of tee-shirt that says, "Jesus Saves" on the back, or bumper stickers. That isn't the idea. He's talking about the style of life."[59] If you have ever chosen to adopt a new style of clothes, you may recall how uncomfortable it is at times. For instance if someone decides to wear boots who has only worn shoes, you see them hobble along flat-footed for a few days until at last they grow accustomed to the new style of footwear. This is precisely what happens when the believer puts on the new man, but the rewards are beyond description.

Yet lest we shun this new style of life, we must be aware that the command to put on Christ is not a suggestion but rather a command. In fact it is the proof that you have been adopted. In Matthew's gospel we read about a King who held a great feast. The parable states the "When the king came in to look over the dinner guests, he saw a man there who was not dressed in wedding clothes, and he said to him, "Friend, how did you come in here without wedding clothes?" And the man was speechless. Then the king said to the servants, "Bind him hand and foot, and throw him into the outer darkness; in that place there will be weeping and gnashing of teeth. For many are called, but few are chosen."[60] Thus it is with urgency that Paul speaks saying, "Do this, knowing the time, that it is already the hour for you to awaken from sleep; for now salvation is nearer to us than when

---

[59] MacArthur, John.
http://www.gty.org/resources/sermons/2147/Putting-on-the-New-Man-Part-1
[60] Matthew 22:12-14

we believed. The night is almost gone, and the day is near. Therefore let us lay aside the deeds of darkness and put on the armor of light. Let us behave properly as in the day, not in carousing and drunkenness, not in sexual promiscuity and sensuality, not in strife and jealousy. But put on the Lord Jesus Christ, and make no provision for the flesh in regard to its lusts."[61]

Here end all the excuses and "I cant's" for the believer. Since God dwells within you, you shouldn't say "I can't live right, I can't forgive, or I can't overcome." Rather you should say with Paul "I can do all thing through Christ who strengthens me."[62] Now you have the power of God at your disposal to live a God honoring life.

A Share of the Inheritance

Finally, we note the third result of this spiritual adoption. The believer in addition to a new identity, and new nature, receives a share in the inheritance of Christ. "If you are a son, then you are an heir of God through Christ."[63] Because "if we are His children, we are heirs also, heirs of God and fellow heirs with Christ, if indeed we suffer with Him so that we may also be glorified with Him."[64]

I recall a story I heard in my childhood. It was told by Pastor John Hagee. It seems a very wealthy man had died and left no heir to his vast estate. This was because the man's sole heir, a son, had died in his youth. The estate was to be auctioned piece by piece and the people came from miles away to bid. The auctioneer opened the auction by placing up for bid a portrait of the estate owner's young son. The portrait had no real value, it was not painted by a great artist. The young man was never famous nor likely to be. The crowds wondered why this worthless portrait was being auctioned first. The room was silent as the auctioneer called for bids. No one seemed interested in the least. Finally a voice was heard from the back of the room. It was a butler who had helped care for the young man before he died. He said, "Sir, I

---

[61] Romans 13:11-14
[62] Philippians 4:13
[63] Galatians 4:7
[64] Romans 8:17

can't afford much. I only have a few dollars to my name. But that young man was very dear to me, and I would be honored to own that portrait which his father loved." The auctioneer accepted the small bid, and then announced that the auction was over. The crowd protested since only one item had been sold, and so many valuable things remained. The auctioneer announced, "According to the will, whoever acquired the portrait of the son, shall be the heir of the entire estate." This is the great reality of our adoption. Because we have acquired the Son by faith, we are heirs of all of God's glorious estate.

Paul wrote to the Corinthians, "So then let no one boast in men. For all things belong to you, whether Paul or Apollos or Cephas or the world or life or death or things present or things to come; all things belong to you, and you belong to Christ; and Christ belongs to God."[65] The believer who grasps this truth, will walk daily in the power of divine supply.

Matthew Henry write that:

"If we belong to Christ, and are true to him, all good belongs to us, and is sure to us. All is ours, time and eternity, earth and heaven, life and death. We shall want no good thing. But it must be remembered, at the same time, that we are Christ's, the subjects of his kingdom, his property. He is Lord over us, and we must own his dominion, and cheerfully submit to his command and yield themselves to his pleasure, if we would have all things minister to our advantage. All things are ours, upon no other ground than our being Christ's. Out of him we are without just title or claim to anything that is good. Note, Those that would be safe for time, and happy to eternity, must be Christ's.[66]

---

[65] 1 Corinthians 3:21-23

[66] Henry, Matthew, and Leslie F. Church. Commentary on the whole Bible: Genesis to Revelation. Grand Rapids, MI: Zondervan Pub. House, 1961. Print.

Jesus the Model Son

Now we have laid the ground work for the doctrine of Spiritual Sonship. Thus far we have noted how the gift comes to exist in a believer's life. Yet the question is still before us. What does it mean to be a son? What is our role in Sonship? I believe that the answer to that question will unlock for you the door to every form of spiritual blessing as well as unlock for you the door of fruitfulness in ministry. Thus, our study must focus on Christ the model son.

Jesus bears the title "Son of God," and the fact that he walked in that sonship so fully is what made his earthly ministry possible. Andrew Murray wrote that "This was the secret to Christ's wonderful life."[67] His model of Sonship should serve as a pattern for us, as well as a motivation.

Lost In The Father's Love

Jesus was the perfect model of Sonship. He was that in eternity past, a time which we have little insight into, but he was more for our benefit in is earthly ministry. I submit to you that this fact arises out of His knowledge of His Father's love. The fact that Jesus walked in the absolute assurance of His Father's affection, made him effective in His earthly ministry. He said to the Jews in John 5:20 "The Father loves the son, and shows Him all things that He Himself is doing."

Again in John 10:17 he writes that "For this reason the Father loves Me, because I lay down My life so that I may take it again." These expressions of the Father's love reveals to us the fact that Jesus knew that His Father loved Him and soaked in that love.

Jesus said "My Father is glorified by this, that you bear much fruit, and so prove to be My disciples. Just as the Father has loved Me, I have also loved you; abide in My love. If you keep My commandments, you will abide in My love; just as I have kept My Father's commandments and abide in His love. These things I have

---

[67] Murry, Andrew. "Like Christ, Thoughts on the Blessed of Conformity to the Son of God" Morrison and Gibb, Edinburgh. Pg 202-209. 1884

spoken to you so that My joy may be in you, and that your joy may be made full."

The word "abide" literally means to "make a constant residence." Jesus made His home, or rather his "constant residence," in the Father's love. He dwelt daily in the zip code of divine affection. From that place of security the Son of God worked the works of God on earth.

This is no small matter for us to consider. Galatians 5:6 teaches that "faith works through love." Our faith will never be activated toward God unless we believe that He loves us. Love is the ground from which faith springs, and until we walk in the knowledge of our Father's love, we will bear little if any fruit. Faith works though love.

If I do not believe that God loves me, I will never ask anything of Him in faith. If I struggle to believe that He loves me, I will scarily believe that he cares enough to hear me let alone answer affirmatively. Yet I have found that when I am most convinced of His affection, I not only pray bigger prayers but I take greater steps of faith.

Condemnation has the opposite effect. When one feels condemned or under judgment, it pushes them away from God. I've never seen a person walking in condemnation also walk in faith.

The Apostle John later writes to his disciples in 1 John 4:18 "And we have come to know and have believed the love which God has for us. God is love, and the one who abides in love abides in God and God abides in Him." John obviously had learned the great joy of making a "constant residence" in the Father's love. The results for John and for us are remarkable. Firstly John points out that "Perfect love cast out fear." Primarily it casts out the fear of judgment. For he states in verse 17 that "Love is perfected with us, that we may have confidence in the day of Judgment."

Condemnation is the fear of Judgment. Yet the love of God gives the sons of God confidence that when they stand before Him in judgment they will have nothing to fear. There is not fear, because their sin has been dealt with at the cross. If one is in

Christ, he need not fear Judgment. For Christ has suffered the wrath of God in our place. And the Love of God made that provision for us. Yet our enemy effectively uses the fear of judgment to neutralize our faith. He uses fear and condemnation as wedges between the Father and his sons. He does this because he knows that if he can get us to believe that God does not love us, that he will neutralize our faith, stop our prayer life, and bring havoc all around.

I once heard a friend of mine say, "I told the Lord that I loved Him, and the Lord said 'Do you really love me?'" When I heard that, I thought "That could not be God." It just didn't fit with my concept of God, nor with my study of Scripture. I was more used to a conversation with God where I said "I love you Lord and He Said 'I love you too.'" It stuck me that my friend was walking under the constant fear of not measuring up. He seemed to have a concept of a God who was perpetually dissatisfied with him and his efforts to please Him.

Having served the body of Christ for this many years, I know that this is a prevailing view of God which many still struggle with. Since guilt and condemnation was the primary tool used to spur many to live rightly, the result was a loveless relationship with God. A relationship which looked more like an employer /employee relationship, than that of a Father and Son.

Yet the Scripture paints a far different picture of God. Jesus has done all the "measuring up" which we will ever need. He has met all the righteous demands of God at the Cross. And in doing so, has introduced us to our Father's love.

God, I am convinced, wants us to know him as our loving Father. When we express our love to Him, he wants us to hear Him say "I love you too." This is more than mere rhetoric on the part of a writer, but it is His expressed will in the Scripture. John wrote "See how great a love the Father has bestowed on us, that we would be called children of God; and such we are."

Not only do we experience freedom from the fear of judgment in the Father's love, but we can know freedom from the fear of the unknown.

History tells of a Minister named George Matheson. He was in love and engaged to a woman until she learned that he developed a condition which ultimately would leave him blind. The rejection crushed his spirit, and the blindness robbed him as well. His sister helped him cope with the blindness until she got married. On the night of her wedding the wound of past disappointment was ripped open yet again as he pondered a life alone. He went into his study and threw himself into the zip code of Divine affection. That night as he made his residence in God's love he wrote the words of this hymn.

> O Love that will not let me go,
> I rest my weary soul in thee;
> I give thee back the life I owe,
> That in thine ocean depths its flow
> May richer, fuller be.[68]

Matheson found freedom from the fear of the unknown in the Father's love.

The earthly ministry of Jesus was rooted in the Father's love. And so must our lives be. Being convinced of the Father's love is the first step of Sonship and the ground of fruitfulness. It is my prayer for you that you may come to the revelation of God's love, and walk in its light. For when you abide in His love "your joy will be made full."

When you walk in the knowledge of God's Love, you will walk in freedom from fear and condemnation. That freedom, frees our faith to work the works of God.

Committed to the Father's Will

Furthermore, we see in the example of Christ that he was perfectly committed to the Fathers will. Time and time again we read in the Gospels the joyful resolve of the Son to do the will of God the Father. He said in John 4:34 "My food is to do the will of Him who sent Me and to accomplish His work." And in John 5: 19 we hear him say "Truly, truly, I say to you, the Son can do nothing

---

[68] Hymn by George Matheson

51

of Himself, unless it is something He sees the Father doing; for whatever the Father does, these things the Son also does in like manner." He never once took the initiative nor acted of his own will. Even as a child of twelve years old in the Temple at Jerusalem we hear him say to Mary and Joseph "I must be about my Father's business." This was no reference to being a carpenter as Joseph was. Rather it was a clarification of his call by God to be what he was from before the incarnation. "Jesus left his father's business in order to pursue his Father's business."[69]

Ultimately the greatest proof of this truth was the cross. The cross was a surrender to the Father's design and from Gethsemane we hear him say "Father, if You are willing, remove this cup from Me; yet not My will, but Yours be done."[70]

The blind hymn writer Fanny Crosby penned a hymn which I think ought to stimulate our own desire to surrender to the Father's will. She wrote "Consecrate me now to Thy service, Lord, By the power of grace divine; Let my soul look up with a steadfast hope, And my will be lost in Thine." The familiar chorus of this song is a plea asking to be brought "nearer, to the cross." This nearness to the cross is key not merely because dying to our own will is important but because it is in surrender that real life begins. When our will is lost in His, then and then alone can significant living begin.

Shaped by the Father's Presence

Furthermore we may note that Jesus was shaped by the Father's presence. He said in John 8:38 "I speak the things which I have seen [a]with My Father; therefore you also do the things which you heard from your Father." This implies that he spent lots of time with the Father. Not only in ages past in pre-incarnate glory, but in His earthly ministry. Often he withdrew alone to a solitary place to pray. It was this time spent in the presence of the Father that gave Jesus his life and effectiveness.

---

[69] McNeal, Reggie. A work of heart: understanding how God shapes spiritual leaders. San Francisco: Jossey-Bass, 2000. Print. pg 57

[70] Luke 22:42

He said in another place "As the living Father sent Me, and I live because of the Father, so he who eats Me, he also will live because of Me." (John 6:57) Because Jesus was shaped by the Fathers life, then that life became life to us. So it is friends that when you and I are lost in the life of God, we will then and only then be capable of giving life to others.

If we ever hope to have effectiveness in ministry, the kind that leaves a mark on people's lives, the sort that shapes people's thinking about God and makes them hungry for Him, that kind of effectiveness draws the apathetic into action, and feeds the hungry. We must be first shaped by the life of God in us. This shaping takes place in the secret place with God.

Summation

A word to the young preacher. The anointing does not flow toward personality and self-promotion. Neither does it flow toward great use of language or rhetoric. The anointing flows toward Sons. It flows toward hearts who highest aim is to be glorifying the Father. God does not look for three-piece suits, or a sports coat with jeans. He isn't looking for style at all. He's looking for yielded hearts, and there is not a heart more yielded than that of a man committed to being a Son.

We suffer in the church today from the lost art of Sonship. The lone ranger mentality has invaded the ranks of clergy to diminishing effect on their fruitfulness. The anointing flows to Sons, and through Sons. God will only use a Son to carry out his work in the world, because He will only use submitted instruments. Please don't make the mistake of thinking that just because you finished your Bible training, you no longer have a need of a Father to teach you. This will sink your ministry quicker than anything else.

If you compare the character of Joseph up against that of His brothers, you will find that Joseph demonstrated the qualities of a true son. While his brothers were older, and had lived with Jacob their father longer than Joseph, it is clear that they never came to know the heart of their father. Note the following examples.

In Genesis 37 Jacob sent his sons to Shechem to pasture his

flocks. Shechem was a rich pasture. It was rich in forage for Jacobs flocks, but it was also rich in spiritual history for Jacob's family. No doubt the boys knew that it was in that valley that Grandpa Abraham had built his first Altar to YHWH. (Genesis 12:6) This was covenant ground. They would also have remembered that it was here in this valley that their father had erected another Altar after he reconciled with their Uncle Esau. (Genesis 33:2) This altar they would have seen firsthand. Yet they left Shechem saying "Let us go the Dothan." Why would they leave this pasture, and go in search of another?

I submit that they left because they did not share their father's heart. Abraham, Isaac, and Jacob were all builders of Altars. Men who loved the Altar, the meeting place with God. They were all imperfect men, who failed and fell short. Yet they all cultivated a passion for communion with YHWH. They understood that the Altar was a place for getting things right, for renewing vital communion, and for vision and revelation. Yet this did not seem to be the heart of Jacob's older sons.

There is another things which happened at Shechem which may shed light on this in a greater way. In Genesis 34, Shechem became the site of a violent atrocity committed by these men in revenge for their sister Dinah. Perhaps this is why they left Shechem. It was a reminder of their sin and they were unwilling to repent or be reminded. Rather than build an altar and discover the God of their Fathers, they said "Let us go to Dothan." Dothan was the Las Vegas of the region, and it's clear that the boys had other ideas. Rather than stay where their father had sent them they went on to pursue course of half obedience. They would pasture their flocks, and yet be close enough to "sin city" to make it worth their while.

These boys demonstrated that while they were Jacob's sons in biology, they were not his Sons in Spirit. Joseph on the other hand, would prove to be a true Son of Jacob in his Spirit toward God.

Being a son is no mere passive experience. It requires an act of our will and a commitment of our heart to know and enjoy the heart of our Father. Jacob loved Joseph more than his brothers, and I contend that it was because He saw in him his own heart. He saw in Joseph the beating of the same heart.

Since Joseph is a type of Christ and a type of the church, it is important that we explore the ways that Jesus modeled Sonship for us, so that as the church we may walk as Sons of God.

Chapter 4

The Coat of Divine Favor

Joseph found favor in his sight and became his personal servant; and he made him overseer over his house, and all that he owned he put in his charge. Genesis 39:4

Joseph's coat of many colors typifies the work of each member of the Godhead in the life of a believer. I will labor over this point in this section to unfold this truth. We believe in the triune Godhead; God the Father, God the Son, and God the Holy Spirit. One God in three eternal persons. Each member of the Godhead possessing equality in nature, power, authority, value, and worth. Yet each revealing distinct functions. My study of the scriptures has helped me to see that the Father wills, the Son executes that will, and the Holy Spirit administers that will. I will give you two brief examples before continuing.

Look with me at the Creation account in Genesis. We see that the Father willed the creation. Then we see that the Son of God was the agent by which that creation came into being. Finally we see that it was the Holy Spirit who administered the creation. Furthermore, we can look at the plan of salvation. It was Fathers will that Salvation come to mankind. The will of the Father was then executed by Christ in his atoning work on the Cross. Finally we know that it is the Holy Spirit who administers salvation to our hearts.

We live in days when denominational preferences can cause us to ignore or emphasize a person of the Godhead. I grew up in a Pentecostal church where the work of the Holy Spirit was greatly emphasized, but little was taught about God the Father or Christ the Son. I studied in a university which had a great emphasis on the Person of Christ, but little emphasis on the work of the Holy Spirit. In either case, God the Father was left out of emphasis.

My purpose in this section is not to emphasize the role of one member of the Godhead above another, and I am quite sure that was not the intention of my church or school. My purpose rather, is to spark within your mind the flame of wonder at the thought that every member of the Godhead can be known, and experienced.

Furthermore, I hope to show you how each member of the Godhead has made provision for your success in your Christian life and ministry. This provision can be known and experienced on a daily basis and is the foundation for effectiveness.

The Father's Favor

Joseph's coat was a symbol to him of the fact that his Father loved him and had shown favor to him. This favor was initially bestowed on Joseph in the physical reality of the coat of many colors. He wore that coat until it was taken from him buy the jealous act of his brother's treachery. While he wore that coat he was daily remained that His father loved him and had favored him above his brothers. The coat was a tangible reminder that Jacob had given him first born status among his brothers. However so long as he wore the coat in the tent of Jacob, he could not enjoy the full measure of the advantage he had been given. Favor is really only truly experienced in a place of adversity, and Joseph would discover that very soon. Additionally, so long as he wore the coat, the spiritual reality of his mantle was concealed by the physical.

The loss of his coat at the hands of his brothers gave Joseph an opportunity to realize that the coat was only a symbol for what rested upon him spiritually. From the day that Jacob dressed his son in that coat, God's blessing was on Joseph whether he was wearing it or not. From that moment on, people in every season of Joseph's life would see the mantle that he wore in his inner man. In the first season of his downturn we find him in the house of Potifar. And we read in Genesis 39:4 " Joseph found favor in his sight and became his personal servant; and he made him overseer over his house, and all that he owned he put in his charge." Note that favor gave Joseph a distinct advantage in three ways.

First, he became the personal servant giving him the advantage of insight. Then he made him overseer, giving him the advantage of leadership experience. Finally he was placed in charge of all of the estate, giving him the advantage of great responsibility. I wonder how many people today think of those things as advantages. But that merely demonstrates the smallness of our modern ambitions. If you only seek advantage to serve yourself, you lose sight of all that God intended from us in the first place. Furthermore, it is doubtful that Joseph would have learned the skills let along the gained position needed to save Egypt or Israel from the coming famine if he has stayed in the tents of Jacob.

In the second scene of his downturn Joseph finds himself in jail. Even there we read that "the LORD was with Joseph and extended kindness to him, and gave him favor in the sight of the chief jailer. The chief jailer committed to Joseph's charge all the prisoners who were in the jail; so that whatever was done there, he was responsible for it. The chief jailer did not supervise anything under Joseph's charge because the LORD was with him; and whatever he did, the LORD made to prosper."[71] Again we see a series of advantages given to Joseph as a result of the favor that rests on his life.

At last Joseph's downturn became an upturn, and yet again the favor of God was upon him. In one day Joseph went from the pit to the palace, and through the interpretation of Pharaoh's

---

[71] Genesis 39:21

dream was promoted to the second place of command in all of Egypt. Pharaoh said to Joseph, "See, I have set you over all the land of Egypt. Then Pharaoh took off his signet ring from his hand and put it on Joseph's hand, and clothed him in garments of fine linen and put the gold necklace around his neck. He had him ride in his second chariot; and they proclaimed before him, "Bow the knee!" And he set him over all the land of Egypt. Moreover, Pharaoh said to Joseph, "Though I am Pharaoh, yet without your permission no one shall raise his hand or foot in all the land of Egypt."[72] Now Joseph will wear the coat of Egypt's favor, because the Favor of God was on his life from the tents of Jacob.

We too have received a coat from God the Father. This is the Coat of Divine Favor. We have received the Grace of God, which is God's unmerited favor toward man. Many people struggle with the idea that God is for them. And for this reason they struggle to enjoy the Grace and Favor of God. It is my hope that as you read this chapter you will discover how much God loves you and how much favor he has shown to you.

Important Points about Favor:

- Favor is God's endorsement.
- The Favor of God will give you the advantage.
- Your dream will never be achieved without the Favor of God.
- The Favor of God will open doors that no one can shut, and shut doors that no one can open.
- Favor is a result, not a coincidence.
- Favor can do in a day what you can't do in a lifetime.
- Favor flows where it is wanted.

Defining the Favor of God

In his book *The Spirit of Favor On Your House,* Pastor Jerry Savell identified the following four definitions of favor.[73]

---

[72] Genesis 42:42
[73] Sevelle, Jerry. The Spirit of Favor on your House. Jerry Savell Ministries, Crowley Texas.

- something granted out of goodwill
- a gift bestowed as a token of regard
- preferential treatment
- an advantage

Each of these definitions help us see the several aspects of favor, and help us understand why we need the God favor in our life. Yet there is one more word I would like to use in defining favor, and that is the word used by the King James Version of the Bible. The King James bible uses the word "grace" in place of the word favor. Grace is literally unmerited favor. To receive grace is to receive something which you did not deserve, nor could you have merited. When we walk in grace, we are walking in what is truly the greatest advantage a human being could possess. This enviable position has been granted to all who will believe in Jesus Christ as Lord. Note from the scripture some of the advantages that God's favor has provided.

The Psalmist describes the results of God's favor saying "For his anger lasts only a moment, but his favor lasts a lifetime; weeping may last for the night, but rejoicing comes in the morning."[74] Notice the contrast of God's wrath which brings weeping but is short lived; to His favor which brings rejoicing and last for a lifetime. This is nothing less than the grace of God. This grace is long lasting and enduring.

The Exodus of the children of Israel from Egypt was a result of God's favor. After four hundred years of bondage, the Egyptians spoiled themselves and handed over their wealth in restitution to Israel. We read in Exodus 3:21 "I will grant this people favor in the sight of the Egyptians; and it shall be that when you go, you will not go empty-handed." There we see that favor will cause even our enemies to cooperate with God's plan for our lives. "God wants to bless us, assist us and give us preferential treatment and special advantages in life. Not only that, but when we are fully enjoying God's favor, he also increases our favor with other people: 'when a man's ways please the LORD, He makes even his enemies to be at peace with him.'"[75]

---

[74] Psalm 30:5
[75] Vander Klok, Duane. Unleashing the Force of Favor. Chosen.

Proverbs 16:15 states that "In the light of a king's face is life, And his favor is like a cloud with the spring rain." God's favor on a life is like the rain which produces fruitfulness and productivity.

Appropriating The Favor of God

The first key is the revelation of the fact that as a child of God, you have divine favor on your life. This is Gods unmerited favor towards you. You cannot earn it, or buy it, only receive it and enjoy it. The Psalmist writes saying "For it is You who blesses the righteous man, O LORD, You surround him with favor as with a shield."[76] This favor is on your life by virtue of that fact that your life is in Christ. So long as you are in Christ, the favor of God that rests on him, rests on you. "Blessed be the God and Father of our Lord Jesus Christ, who has blessed us with every spiritual blessing in the heavenly places in Christ."[77] Note the key word there is that we have every spiritual blessing "in Christ." For some reason this is hard for us to accept sometimes. But its acceptance is essential to its enjoyment.

Paul uses an even more emphatic phrase in his letter to the Corinthians saying, "Let no one boast in men. For all things belong to you, whether Paul or Apollos or Cephas or the world or life or death or things present or things to come; all things belong to you, and you belong to Christ; and Christ belongs to God."[78] He says "all things belong to you." The preacher in the pulpit along with the promises he preaches belong to you. The "world" and all that's in it belongs to you. That means a house to live in, food to eat, cloth to wear. It means the job you have, the schooling you need, and everything in the world that you need to achieve God's purpose for your life, belongs to you. Life belongs to you. Eternal life[79] in the ages to come. Abundant life[80] in this hear and now. A life you

---

Rapid City, Michigan.
[76] Psalm 5:12
[77] Ephesians 1:3
[7878] 1 Corinthians 3:21-22
[79] 1 John 5:13
[80] John 10:10

love[81] and enjoy rather than loath and tolerate belongs to you. Even death belongs to you. "Where oh death is your victory and grave where is your sting.?"[82] For even death serves you as a bridge to eternal life, and whether you live or die with Christ it is gain.[83] The present is yours. Present opportunities, present resources, and desires. Everything you need to do God's will today, is yours today. And the future is yours too. Nothing you will need in the future will be left out of God's plan. The power to walk in your dreams and fulfill divine design is yours. And this is so, because you belong to Christ, and Christ belongs to God.

We hear in this the echoes of the Father's words to the Elder brother in the Parable of the Prodigal Son. "My child you have always been with me, and all that is mine is yours."[84] The elder brother never rebelled, never left home, but neither did he ever enjoy his father's favor. He had not apprehended the fact that the whole estate was his to enjoy. So you see, the problem is not in the truth of the statement that all things belong to us, rather in the appropriation of that truth in our life.

---

[81] 1 Peter 3:10
[82] 1 Corinthians 15:55
[83] Philippians 1:21
[84] Luke 15:31

Chapter 5

Positioned For Favor

Then she fell on her face, bowing to the ground and said to him, "Why have I found favor in your sight that you should take notice of me, since I am a foreigner?" Boaz replied to her, "All that you have done for your mother-in-law after the death of your husband has been fully reported to me, and how you left your father and your mother and the land of your birth, and came to a people that you did not previously know. May the LORD reward your work, and your wages be full from the LORD, the God of Israel, under whose wings you have come to seek refuge." Then she said, "I have found favor in your sight, my lord, for you have comforted me and indeed have spoken kindly to your maidservant, though I am not like one of your maidservants." Ruth 2:10-13

The Book of Ruth is a very significant book in the history of the nation of Israel. In fact, Ruth is one of the great, great, great grandmothers of Jesus Christ. Although her story occurs several hundred years after that of Joseph, she serves as a model for obtaining the favor of God. Her story like that of Joseph is one of finding the position of favor, while being in adverse and contrary circumstances.

When the story begins, we find her father-in-law and Naomi, and they are living in Bethlehem. The opening chapter of the Book of Ruth tells us that the name of the man was Elimelek and the name of his wife was Naomi. They lived in Bethlehem which is a most significant city in Bible history. It was to become the hometown of Ruth's great grandson King David, and of course the birthplace of the Messiah. The word Bethlehem literally means the house of bread. So they were living in a place of plenty but things took a turn for the worse. In this land of plenty, there was a severe famine. So this family, they packed up their things and they left for another region called Moab, in search of relief.

I want to point out that sometimes even when you are in the middle of the place where God wants you to be, there are going to be difficulties. I know we all wish that the moment we decide to serve Christ, that we find ourselves on easy street and that we are coasting toward heaven without any single difficulty. But you see, our faith will never grow apart from difficulties. Our faith and relationship with God will never develop apart from life's occasional complications.

On one occasion, Jesus said to the disciple let's go fellows, let's get on the boat. They were going to the other the side of the sea of Galilee. That night, they were caught up in a great storm. Did he not know that there was a storm coming? Didn't he know that there was going to be a problem on the sea? Was it that the Lord forgot to check weather.com to make sure that there was going to be smooth sailing that night. No. He wanted the disciples to experience that storm. Because only through that storm, could they witness his power over the wind and the sea.

I know it sounds hard but sometimes God designs a storm just for you. Have you ever been in that moment, in that circumstance where that storm had your name all over it. It was coming straight for you. And there was no way to get out of its path.

I heard the story once of a man and his wife who took a cruise manned by a captain they knew very well One night on board the cruise ship found itself tossed about by a severe storm. The lady called her friend the captain and scolded him for taking this course. She said "If you knew there was going to be a storm why didn't you choose another course." The captain politely replied "You best go on to bed, and get some rest. Tomorrow morning you will wake up at port on time and on schedule. I know this boat, and I know that this boat was made for this storm." When you go through one of life's storms, just remember that God made your ship for that storm.

Naomi's family, they did not do what they should have done. They should have battened down and become firm and let this famine pass but instead they left the place of God's blessing and left behind the House of Bread. They went to place that was foreign to them, with foreign gods, foreign foods, and a foreign language. It was a place that was not designed for them because they were trying to outrun the storm, they were trying to outrun the test. But everyone knows that when you skip a test on Friday, the test is going to be waiting for you on Monday morning.

The Bible tells us that they went into Moab and their two sons took wives. One son married a Moabite woman named Orpah, not Oprah, but Orpah. The other girl's name was Ruth. Things seem like they were going well. Two weddings in Moab were a blessing. Then they had a funeral in Moab, and the father dies. Then before long the sons die too. All that had been accumulated in Moab began to fall as sand through Naomi's hands. She found the tragic and bitter experience that those who leave the will of God cannot expect the blessing of God.

Friends, I want you to know that God's blessing, is at God's house. The blessing of God is in the presence of God. "Those that be planted in the house of the LORD shall flourish in the courts of our God."[85] In verse 8 of chapter 1 we read that Naomi said to her two daughters-in-law, "Go, return each of you to mother's house and may the Lord deal kindly with you as he has dealt with the dead and with me. May the Lord grant you that you may find rest each in the house of her husband." Then she kissed them and lifted up her voice and wept, and they said to her, "No, but we will surely return with you to your people." Naomi said, "Return my daughters, why should you go with me, have I yet sons in my womb that you may find your husbands? Return my daughters, go, for I am too old to have a husband." So Naomi takes these two girls and she said, "You've got to go home because I am going back to Bethlehem. I am going back to the house of bread."

---

[85] Psalm 92:13

This is the first lesson I want us to learn from the Book of Ruth. That the best thing you can do when you have taken a wrong turn is go back to the place where you got off-track.

Return to Bethlehem

"Return to me says the Lord and be saved for I am God and there is no other." These days we have a global positioning system in our cars. It is called GPS. We have that device that says go right and go left. I believe the GPS of the Christian, the global positioning of the Christian, is the Holy Spirit. He says to those who have taken a wrong turn, "Go back to the place of blessing." He says to you and I, "Come back to the presence of God, go back to Bethlehem."

Orpah makes her way back to her mother's house but Ruth, Ruth clings to Naomi. She says. "I am not going to leave you. I am not going to leave you, your God will be my God and your family will be my family and where you lodge, I will lodge and where you die, there I will die." She clung to Naomi because she knew that maybe Naomi had taken a wrong turn, but that the Jewish people were a blessed people.

Ruth knew that Naomi might have been in trouble, she might have been in distress, but she had a big God who was able to turn things around. And now rumor had it that the famine had ended and that the blessing and prosperity of God had returned to Bethlehem. She began to understand "I have got to get home. I have got to go back to the place where I used to be, that place with God, that place of blessing."

I believe we are hearing similar rumors and the rumblings and roaring of a move of God that is descending upon the church of the 21st Century. I believe we are hearing the rumors and the rumblings and roaring of the storm clouds gathering over a hungry people, to pour out the showers of divine blessing, and the deluge God's spirit upon us again.

Every Season Has An End

The second lesson that we can draw from this account is that no season ever lasted forever. Every season has a beginning and it has an end. You may be in a season of plenty today. You may be in a season of abundance and I admonish you to make wise choices about your resources because someday you may a season of famine. If you have done what is wise, then you will be able to overcome. Bible tells us that even the ants store up for the winter.

If you are in a season of plenty, a season of prosperity, then be aware of that difficult day yet to come. I wish the good times would roll forever, but history and scripture advise us that they will not. To the young man, young lady I say, take advantage of your youth for the day will come when you will no longer have the ability to fall down and get up quite so quickly. The day will come when you will not be able to run the mile so fast. The day will come when you will not have the energy and the strength that you have now, so while you have it serve God; while you have it, give it to God, invested in the Kingdom of God, make full use of your time.

I have sat with many men, in different countries around the world and some have wept and said, "Brother Isaac, I wish I had served God as a young man, I wish I had given him my youth, I wish I had given him my vigor and my strength." This too shall pass. Right now, you feel you are immortal, it seems as though you will never die. Seems like you break a bone and it just heals up right quick. But this too shall pass. That season will end.

Maybe you are middle aged and you no longer have the time or the energy you had when you were a teenager or in college but you too can make use of this season; because it will also pass. You perhaps are in that season of raising children; raise them for the glory of God. Maybe you are in a time where you can work and amass more wealth. Make hay while the sun shineth my friend, for this will pass as well. If you are in the silver age of life, you are in the older years, live them for the glory of God for this too shall pass.

I was told this parable while on the mission field in Chile. It's not at all biblical but it is a keen insight into man's life. . The story says that God was making a donkey one day and he said to the donkey, "You are going to work all the days of your life and I am going to give you 35 years of labor." The donkey said, "God I will do whatever you tell me to do, 35 years however is a long time, just give me 10 or 15." God said alright.

69

Then God created a dog and said, "I am going to make you loyal, you are going to stick around your master's home and protect it, you will sit on the front porch and bark when the enemy comes and I am going to give to 30 years." The dog said, "Oh God I will do whatever you say. Just do not give me 30 years for that is too long." God gave him the years that he wanted.

Then God created a monkey and he said, "You are not going to have much of a home, you're just going to bounce around from tree to tree and I am going to give you 30 years." The monkey said, "God I will do whatever you want me to do but do not give me 30 years as that is a long time."

Finally, God made man. He said, "You are the choices of my creation. I am going to give to 30 years to live." The man said, "God I will do whatever you want but 30 years is not long enough, why don't you give me the years the donkey did not want and the years that the dog didn't want and the years that the monkey didn't want." God said, "Alright." And that say the Chileans is why man works like a donkey for 30 years laboring by the sweat of his brow. Then, once he retires he stays home like a loyal dog, sitting on the front porch protecting the house, mostly delighted by any guest. When he gets very old, he is more like a monkey bouncing around from house to house with his children, staying wherever he can.

What season are you in? If you are in the donkey's season, work while you can. If you are in the old yeller season, love your grandchildren while you can. If you are in a monkey's season, be a good guest. And in all seasons be grateful for the length of your days, for they too shall pass.

We spoke of the ages of life and we spoke about the season of prosperity but what if you are in a season of financial difficulties? What if you are in a season of ill-health, or a season of setbacks? Where your dreams seemed to disappear and the wait for a breakthrough turned out to be discouragingly long.

My friend, this season also will pass. Every season has an end and I admonish you to hold on, like Ruth held on to Naomi. Hold on to God and follow the Lord Jesus Christ. Hold on to the faith bound in the pages of the Holy Bible, hold on to what you have learned, hold on to what you have been taught. Whatever the season may be, whatever the trial, the circumstance, the setback, the fear or concern, trust Him; he is the author of every season. These difficult days too shall pass. You and I may not know what the future holds but we know who holds the future and He is the author of our lives. Here in His divine providence, God took the mistake, the wrong turn and the bad decisions of Elimelek and Naomi. And turned it into an opportunity.

An opportunity to bring a gentile young lady named Ruth into the Jewish nation. This failure of Elimelek and Naomi should have been for ruin but it turned out to be for blessing, it turned out to be for the prosperity of the nation of Israel; it turned out to be for our blessing because Ruth is in our spiritual family tree. And she is there not because she was better than anybody else, not because she was more attractive than anybody else, not because she had a better resume than anybody else, but simply because she stuck with God.

Have you left Bethlehem? If so, it's the time to return. Have you left word; it's the time to return. Have you left the place of prayer; it's the time to return. Are you in a season you can't wait to end, you never know. You may make that season longer or shorter, based upon how you respond to it. If you complain and say "Why God?" then you will just go around the cycle again. Or you can say, "God I don't understand but I trust you. I don't like the situation but I trust you."

A Day of Favor

Ruth is a picture or type of the Church of the Lord Jesus Christ. She was not a Jewish girl, she had no Jewish roots and she was a stranger to the convent of Israel. She was in fact a Moabite. The Moabites had a sorted history with Israel to say the least. This meant she was a gentile and the Jews had no regard for gentiles. We see how God takes a gentile girl and makes her part of the family tree of the Messiah.

As we look at Ruth, we can think of looking at ourselves, the gentile Church who was given favor and position in the family of God. The Bible says that Jesus came to his own, but his own received him not. But to those that received him that is you and I, the gentiles. To them he gave the right to be called the sons of God.

As we look at Ruth I want you to see yourself and then ask yourself some very important questions. How did Ruth received the favor of God? How is that she was able to secure the favor of God? In answering these questions, we will see how it is that you and I can have the favor of God. And then I want you to apply those principles to your life.

Ruth and Naomi were in the lowest class. They were the poorest of the poor and upon returning, Naomi said to Ruth, "I want you to go and find a field where you glean. See if you can bring some grain home so that we can eat." You see, there was a rule in ancient Israel regarding the poor. This was an ancient welfare system, except very different from ours. If a farmer had a field of barley or wheat, the whole field was his, of course. But he was required to leave the four corners of the field untouched. Those four fields were left so that the poorest of the poor could go and collect enough grain to eat.

So, it was not that they were receiving a check, but rather they had go and harvest the barley themselves. Furthermore, the rule stated that as the reaper was reaping if a grain or two would fall from his bundle he was not allowed to go back and it pick up. What he had dropped was left behind for the poor. The poor would come in late in the afternoon after the bundles have been tied and pick up what was left and this was called "gleaning".

Ruth takes the initiative to go and glean. We notice here again the character of Ruth. And the way that her character positions her for favor. She was humble enough to glean, honoring enough to go instead of the aged Naomi, and industrious enough to find a way forward.

Humility Attracts Favor

Gleaning though lawful, was a beggar's lot. It certainly wasn't something that people would be proud to do. Yet if you were too proud to glean you may well end up starving. So we see the humility of Ruth, willing to take the lowest place available to make ends meet. The scripture says that God gives "grace (favor) to the humble, but He resists the proud." Pride will hinder favor in ways one cannot fully calculate. For God to "resist" someone literally means he "sets himself against them." The proud are pushing a boulder uphill with God pushing down against them. There is no way around divine resistance.

I am convinced that pride will stop favor faster than any other character issue in your life. John Ruskin states "all other passions do occasional good; but whenever pride puts in its word, everything goes wrong." There is a high cost to pride and the record of scripture is clear. Because of pride Nebuchadnezzar was stuck on stupid for seven years. Pride led Rehoboam to lose the unity of the Kingdom of Israel. Even godly King Uzziah became a leper because of pride.

But humility is a magnet for divine aid. The Lord said in Isaiah "I dwell on a high and holy place, And also with the contrite and lowly of spirit In order to revive the spirit of the lowly And to revive the heart of the contrite." If you wish to be positioned for divine favor, take the path of humility. Whoever exalts himself shall be humbled; and whoever humbles himself shall be exalted. Matthew 23:12 If in fact "pride comes before the fall," then humility must precede promotion. Ruth, unknowingly by taking the low road has positioned herself for favor.

Hard Work Attracts Favor

Another aspect of Ruth's character which we cannot dispense with is her work ethic. Scripture states that she gleans "from morning until night." All day she gleaned in that field, making use of her time. She could have stayed home hoping for opportunity to knock, but instead she set out to find opportunity. I fear that we are seeing the rise of a generation who has been so accustomed to advantage and prosperity that it has not learned the value of industry. The value of doing something in pursuit of purpose. The psalmist wrote about the righteous man saying "whatsoever he does will prosper."

Ruth was walking in the light of this very important principle. God will bless what you do! He will not bless what you plan to do. Hope to do. Would like to do. Might do. He will bless what you do. Ruth had to do something. This not only positioned her for success but also for the favor of God. The truth is that whether it's finding a way to survive an economic downturn, or pursuing Gods dream for our lives, there is a definite demand for action.

In his book on *Making Ideas Happen* Scott Belsky talks about the need to have an organizational bias toward action. I think he is right, and has tapped into a truth revealed in scripture from long ago. It seems to me that God has built into the creation a "bias toward doing." For some reason we often assume the position of "waiting on God." And what's more, we assume that this is a highly spiritual posture. The fact is that waiting on God really means trusting in God. It has nothing to do with watching God do everything we need done.

Now I understand that there are seasons for waiting for God's answer, timing, provision, or supply. But it's an altogether different and misguided notion that expects God to do the "doing." God didn't build the Ark, the Tabernacle, or rebuild Jerusalem. In every case he used human agents to "do" his will. So it might just be that instead of waiting on God, God is actually waiting on you.

The Providence of God

Trusting in God's providence, Ruth sets out to find a place to glean. Ruth finds herself on the fields of a wealthy well-respected Jew named Boaz. He was the very man that is going to be the source of God's favor towards her. You should know something about the providence of God. God is able to superintend every detail of your life, and there are no accidents. Ruth may have thought that by chance she arrived at a good field to glean, but there was no chance in this matter.

It was God who had established a point and a place at which He would bring survival and blessing to the family of Naomi. Not only does Ruth happen upon the right field, but she did so at the right time. It turns out that the landowner was there as well. Had she been in the right field at the wrong time, he never would have noticed her. Had she been in the wrong field at the right time, favor would have passed her by. But she is in Gods providence in the right place at the right time.

When Boaz saw Ruth, she instantly found favor in his sight.

He said to her, "I want you to pick whatever you want out of this field. Don't go to any other fields to glean. You can even drink out the employee's water buckets over there. If you get thirsty, you just go help yourself to the employee lounge and get whatever you need. And when you see my workers move onto another field, follow them there too."

Ruth was instantly aware that she was being given preferential treatment. And so she asked the all-important question. "Why have I found favor in your sight that you should take notice of me since I am a foreigner?" The answer to that question is worthy of note, because it is our blueprint for receiving the favor of God.

So, he answered her in verse 11, "All that you have done for your mother-in-law after the death of your husband has been fully reported to me and how you left your father and mother in the land of your birth and came to people that you did not previously know."

Compassion Invites Gods Favor

Here is what brought favor to Ruth's life. It was her compassion for people in the hour of their need. She had compassion for Naomi in her deepest crisis. And rather than say "I'm out of here," she said, "whereever you go, I'll go." I'm going to stick to you.

You and I are called upon by God to be a compassionate Church, to be a loving Church. It is a hard thing sometimes to love those that others do not love, to care for those that others do not care for. Yet without a doubt we see that God put his favor upon those who show kindness to those in need. I have had several conversations in my Pastorate that go like this: "Pastor I have noticed a difference in my personal finances since we began to give to missionary causes." I usually smile and remind them that God honors those who show compassion.

You see, God always favors those who put him first. I am not trying to tell you that missions is the goose that lay the golden egg. But I want you to know that when you put the heart of God up above everything else and you invest in the kingdom of God, you can expect the favor of God upon your life.

If you were able to get up close to the heart of God; close enough to hear the rhythm of his heartbeat, I think you would hear "souls, souls, souls." When you invest in souls, you are showing compassion for those in the greatest need of their life, the need of a savoir and God will put His favor upon you.

God favors those who show compassion to those in need. You may say, "Pastor Isaac, I do not have a lot to give." Neither did Ruth. In fact, she had nothing to give and yet what little she had she was generous with and God put favor on her life. Do you want favor on the job, do you want favor in the home, do you want favor in the market place? Then you must learn to give. If you are a tither, you know what it is like to have the favor the God on your finances.

Isn't it amazing how you can look at the last week or month and you just know you do not enough money and yet by the end of the week somehow, someway all the bills got paid. Why? Because God puts his favor upon those who trust him and believed him and invest in his kingdom.

And then we see that Boaz says to Ruth "May the Lord reward your work and your wages be full from the Lord." This is my prayer for you that your wages will be full from the Lord. My prayer for you is that every time you get a divine paycheck, you say "Wow that is better than I expected. God's favor is on my life. God's favor is on my relationships. God's favor is on my finances."

Favor To Those Who Take Refuge

Now we come to another reason for the favor of God in the life of Ruth. We read in the text "May the Lord reward your work and your wages be full from the Lord, the God of Israel under whose wings you have come to seek refuge." She had taken refuge in the Lord.

If you want the favor of God, you have to have the covering of God. What does it mean to have the covering of God? It means that we submit to him. The prayers Jesus taught us to pray, "Not my will but thine be done."

Ruth knew one thing at least. She knew that if she would find refuge under the wings of Jehovah, that she would be saved. No one from outside would look at the Jewish law and say I want to obey that. The Jewish law was more than 600 precepts and requirements. There were laws on what to eat, laws for how to use the outhouse. There were laws about how to get a job, laws about everything under the sun and yet she does not renege or say I do not want to be a part of this system. Rather, she knows that the God of Israel was a blesser. That the God of Israel was one who will lift up and built up those who trusted in Him and she said I want to hide and submit to the will of the God of Israel. She sought refuge under his wings.

Are you better off today than you were the day that you were living out from under the covering God? Are you better off today than you were when you were going from the nightclub to pub and the bar? Are you better off today than you were when you were trying to find happiness at the bottom of a bottle? Oh I know you can tell me, "Yes pastor I am blessed today. I am better off today than I ever was because I have found refuge under the wings of the God of Israel."

Submission means obedience. We say not my timing, but Yours; not my way or the path that I chose, but Yours. We say my thoughts are much lower than your thoughts. I want to do it your way God. She found favor because she sought refuge under His wings.

Favor Because She Was In The Right Field

Ruth found favor with God and with Boaz because she was at the right field. I want you to note this carefully because you and I have to be at the right field if we want to have the favor of God. You see, you are not going to find the favor of God in Buddha's field. You are not going to find the favor of YHWH in Islam's field. You are not going to find the favor of God at the Republican's field or the Democrat's field. The favor of God is in God's field.

There are many ways we can say this, but the Bible tells us in the Book of Deuteronomy that we can expect the blessing when we bring our offering to Mountain of the Lord. We come to the place that He has chosen, we come to the Church that He has chosen for us, we come to His book which He has chosen. The favor of God is in the field that God has chosen.

Jesus Christ is the field that God has chosen. Jesus Christ is the one and only place where you can find the blessing of God. Sometimes we want the blessing of God but we do not want to go where God tells us to go. We do not want to live the way God tells us to live. We want to have it our own way but we want God to bless us, we want God to pour out His favor upon us. We do not have the right attitude. Often, we do not have the right spirit. We are arrogant before God. We are unwilling to humble ourselves before God and yet we say Lord I have got a light bill and I wish you to pay it.

The Bible tells us God is not mocked. What a man sows that will he also reap. You sow the field with flesh, you are going to get the fruit of the flesh. You sow to the field with the spirit and you are going to reap the fruits of the spirit in your life. So if you want the favor of God, you have ask yourself, "Am I working the God field, am I in the right place?" If you are in the right place and hang tight, even when it seem like everything has fallen apart.

Bethlehem means house of bread and yet a famine came to Bethlehem. A famine came to the house of bread and rather than hold on to the place that God had chosen for Naomi and her family, she left and when she left the place that God had chosen, calamity came upon her and upon her family.

Being in the field which God has chosen doesn't mean you will never have trouble. It does not mean that there is never going to be a storm. It does not mean that there is never going be a hardship. What it does mean is if you hold on and if you trust God, you will see the reward of your patience and the reward of your endurance. So Ruth discovered that she found the favor of God because she went to the place where God had put his hand.

Unexpected Sources of Favor

Note the following two examples of the favor of God. The favor of God came to Ruth unexpectedly, at least she was not expecting it. She was not even looking for it. She was just following the best information she had and she went right to where God wanted her to be. We say, "God I do not have all the answers. I do not know if I should take job A or job B. I do not know if I should buy the house or wait. I do not know if I should sell the car or wait, but I am going to wait on you, you lead me, you guide me." You are doing like Ruth, waiting on God to favor you. He will lead you, he will guide you, he will guard you and even if you make a mistake, he will set it right. She found the favor of God unexpectedly.

The nation of Israel found the favor of God from an unexpected source. You may recall that they were about to leave the nation of Egypt. The Great Passover was done. Pharaoh's hammer fist had finally being broken. They had worked 400 years without a salary, generation after generation in slavery and they are about to leave the nation of Egypt and they are glad just to have the shirt on their back. They are glad just to have something to put their shoes in and belt on and as they were walking out of the nation of Egypt. Egyptians were coming to them and giving them gold, silver, and precious stones.

Usually when an army sacks or spoils a nation they have to go into every house and break down every door, go in and spoil the treasures. But not in this case. The nation of Egypt spoiled itself and they brought to the beleaguered and slave nation their wealth. That day the nation of slaves walked out richer than the Egyptians. They had worked for every last cent that they had earned in those fields. Their work for Pharaoh was returned to them in a single day of favor. Why? Because God gave them his favor in an unexpected place and from an unexpected source.

Maybe you have been through hell and back in this season of your life. Fear not because that season will end, you are going to leave Egypt with our hands full of blessing. The Lord says put me first, take a refuge under my wings, get into my field and you will walk out of Egypt. You will not be owed anything because I will have blessed you and I will have given you everything that belongs to you.

My grandfather used to say "God does not pay every Friday but when he pays, he pays well." It has been said about the wicked, that the mill of God grinds slowly and yet exceedingly small, but I want to say about the righteous. God does not pay every Friday, my friend. But when he gives his wages, they are full.

Boaz pulled a servant aside and said to him, do you see that girl, the gentile. When you are going down the row, I want you to pull out a handful of wheat on purpose, and leave it on the ground in front of her. Get a little further down, pull out another handful on purpose. Get it a little further down, another handful on purpose. So there goes Ruth expecting one or two stocks of grain to glean and all of a sudden she finds the golden handful. And then another and then yet another. She could hardly carry everything home. Naomi said, "What in the world did you do? I do not know, she replies! All I know is that when I gleaning there was more wheat than I could carry, they were hands full at a time."

I want you to be encouraged that it may seem as though sometimes God gives to us a handful and each little handful is meant to encourage. Do not give up, do not quit, do not throw in the towel. Weeping may endure for the night but joy is coming in the morning. God will give you His wages in full.

Chapter 6

Fit
For The
Palace

But Daniel resolved not to defile himself with the royal food and wine, and he asked the chief official for permission not to defile himself this way. Now God had caused the official to show favor and compassion to Daniel. Daniel 1:8-9

The Favor of God will often bring promotion, as it did in the life of Joseph. What we do when promotion happens is perhaps a more important question than how you obtained it. Because getting promoted and staying promoted are different matters. Proverbs 18:16 states that "A man's gift makes room for him, And brings him before great men." This is what happened to Joseph. His gifts had opened doors for him. Even in a foreign nation and under duress the gifts of divine favor had promoted him.

When the day of promotion came for Joseph he was called out of the Prison because the favor of God was resting on his life, and because his gifts had made room for him. Scripture states that when he was summoned to Pharaoh's courts Joseph "shaved himself and changed his cloths."[86] This detail though small raises the issue which I will elaborate in this chapter, that favor will open doors, but we must be equipped to seize them when they open. Your gifts of favor will make room for you too, and will bring you before great men. But you should understand that there is more this than just getting in the door.

In my own life I have experienced this promise many times. I experienced this as an intern in Washington DC. The spring of 2003 I had to opportunity to serve in the Office of the Majority Leader of the House of Representatives. This was an incredible honor for a kid from a small Texas community called Choate. I had the privilege of meeting the greatest men in Congress. I was blessed to meet some of my political heroes, and some rivals. I even met the famed Hilary Clinton, and rode the Senate Subway with Senator Ted Kennedy. You will forgive all the name dropping.

The highlight of the whole experience happened on the second day on the job. It was the 2003 State of the Union Address. President Bush was preparing for War in Iraq and Washington was tense with anticipation. I was the low man on the totem pole, two days on the job, and a lowly unpaid intern to bout. Yet I had the audacity to pray for a seat. I had no chance of a seat in that chamber. Most Congressman only receive two tickets, and the Leader's office had five. And those seats had been given to a foreign delegation.

Since I wasn't going to get a seat, I opted for the next big thing. They told us if you want to go home early you may, but if you want to stay in the Capital Office you may. I figured watching the speech in the office would at least be more fun than watching it in my apartment. And at least I'd get to experience the ambiance of the capital at that momentous occasion. With only minutes to go before the speech, my coworker named John walked in the office. His face was filled with fright, as he walked past my desk and said "Isaac, I think I'm about to get fired." His job was to escort the delegates to their seats.

---

[86] Genesis 41:14

"The foreign delegates refused to go through security and walked off into the night," he said. John walked into the Chief of Staff's office, and I started to pray. I should have been praying that he wouldn't lose his job. But instead I was praying that I would get a ticket. I knew seats were now available, and I asked God for "divine favor."

The chief of staff came out of his office, a very relieved John walked out with him. He said to the other intern still in the office and me, "I don't know how to tell you this guys. Pick a number one through ten. One of you is going to the State of the Union." I blurted out "seven" without a single thought. My colleague had not time to guess. The Chief said "seven it is," and he handed me the ticket. John and I looked at each other and darted into the Capital corridor making our way to the House Chamber.

We sat that night in the gallery of the United States House of Representatives for the State of the Union Address. I still can't believe it even as I write this. I had the opportunity that night to sit in the House Chamber with Senators, Congressman, Supreme Court Judges, and the President of the United States. That may not seem to be a big deal to many, but for a boy from Choate that was the honor of a lifetime. That night favor made room for me, and literally put me in the same room with great men.

The problem with our reading the Proverbs 18:16 promise isn't that it won't happen. Our gifts will make room for us, and they will put us before great men. But what's also true is that often we are not necessarily prepared for such an opportunity. Many people have spoiled the opportunity due to lack of preparation for the occasion. For this reason Solomon also writes saying:

Do not claim honor in the presence of the king, And do not stand in the place of great men; For it is better that it be said to you, "Come up here," Than for you to be placed lower in the presence of the prince, Whom your eyes have seen. Proverbs 25:6-7

Do not be in a hurry to leave the Kings presence. Do not join in an evil matter, for he will do whatever he pleases. Ecclesiastes 8:3

While our gifts may open door for us, poor preparation can close those doors or render them fruitless. There is a protocol in the palace which you do well to learn. Daniel was about to walk onto a platform of incredible influence. His voice would be heard by the King of Babylon. His insight would bless the Empire. Yet he first needed to be prepared for the opportunity.

A mentor once told me, "Isaac, when you are in the presence of someone great ask good questions, then be quiet and let them speak." This has served me greatly in life. And I feel that I've learned a great deal from the strategy. Yet I've also been at dinner at times with someone who I consider great. And inevitably there is someone at the table who doesn't know anything about anything. And yet won't stop talking. You wish you could say to them "Would you please be quiet. We want to hear from the guy who actually has accomplished something." Of course I've never said that, but I confess to thinking it.

So here is some sound advice. Get around people who know more than you do. Who have gone further than you have. Who are older than you are. People who have thought through great questions, and who have learned from past mistakes. People who have a track record of faithfulness. Ask good, profound, introspective questions, and then be quiet and listen. It's hard to learn when you are doing all the talking.

Never assume that just because the door opened, you have all it takes. Humility dictates a different path. One that recognizes that entering the presence of a king is not like hanging out with your friends. Whether the opportunity is before a King, President, Governor or small town mayor. Whether you stand before a donor who has ability to fund your dream. Or you go before an official who can issue permits to build that dream. Know the protocol of that palace, and remember you represent the Kingdom of Heaven. Remember that those in authority hold that authority from God. When you honor them you honor God. For this reason Paul wrote:

"Every person is to be in subjection to the governing authorities. For there is no authority except [b]from God,   and those which exist are established by God. ... Render to all what is due them: tax to whom tax is due; custom to whom custom; fear to whom fear; honor to whom honor.   Romans 13:1-7

One of the clearest models of this is found in the book of Daniel. Like Joseph, Daniel would find himself in the palace of the mightiest king in the world of his day. From the hills of Judea to the courts of Babylon, Daniels gifts would make room for him and bring him before great men. From his story we can learn a few lessons about how to obtain and retain promotion.

Daniel understood this very important principle. God's favor follows honor. If he had not honored the protocol of the Palace, and the Kings demands for preparation, he would have surly shut the door. But because he honored the protocol of the palace, even wider doors opened for him.

Ultimately God's call on my life lead me away from a life in politics. But my time there exposed me to this principle first-hand. Just as in Babylon, there is a protocol in Washington which makes or breaks successful leaders. The protocol of the United States Capital is filled with many unspoken rules. From dress code, to discretion, the time I served made me aware of one basic principle. Adapting to the standard of the palace is essential for success. The palace you enter may not be Babylon or Washington, but where ever it is, honoring the standards will be essential.

The Standards of the Palace

King Nebuchadnezzar did not build Babylon into a world force of philosophical, cultural, and intellectual might by accident. He was very intentional about his objectives. A practice later adopted by Alexander the Great, refined by Nebuchadnezzar. He ensured that the culture of Babylon was infused into every nation he conquered, and set the highest standards for cultural refinement within his government. This idea is one that every leader should understand, that excellence is the result of intentionality, not happenstance.

We have a glimpse into Nebuchadnezzar's standards in Daniel chapter one. After invading the Nation of Judah the Babylonian issued the order that the best and brightest of the Jews be taken captive to Babylon and prepared for service in his government.

The famed bible commentator Matthew Henry explains that this was done for three reasons. First of all, he did this to use the young men as trophies of his conquest. Secondly, he did this to use them as hostages by which to ensure the loyalty of their parents to his government. Thirdly, Nebuchadnezzar would benefit from the best of Israel for his governments longevity and success.

While it may seem like a tragic turn for these young men to be taken to Babylon as exiles, the fact is that they were being given an extraordinary opportunity. The Palace of Nebuchadnezzar would afford them a platform of influence which they never had before. Everyone has a palace into which some day they must enter. Joseph's palace was the courts of Pharaoh. David's Palace was the court of King Saul. Isaiah's Palace was the court of Hezekiah. Nehemiah's palace was the court of Artaxerxes. But there are some palaces that don't look like palaces.

Simply put, a palace is a place of influence; you can make a difference for God. Places of influence which do not include kings or royalty. Maybe like Peter on the day of Pentecost your palace is the local church. Maybe like Boaz your palace is a barley field. Maybe like Joshua your palace is a slave nation on the banks of the Jordan. Whatever your palace is, it's going to demand something from you. There are qualifications for the palace.

Daniel 1:3-4 gives us a list of the qualifications for those chosen. They were to be "of the royal line, without blemish, good looking, intelligent in every branch of wisdom, endowed with understanding, discerning knowledge, and ultimately teachable." The king wanted the best at his service, and in return offered these young men an opportunity to excel. The first six qualifications teach us about getting to the palace. The seventh teaches us how to stay in the Palace.

Royal Blood

The first gift Nebuchadnezzer was looking for was "royal blood." He was looking for men who were princes of Israel. You might say "Well that counts me out." And since we don't acknowledge titles of nobility in the United States no one really does qualify by that standard. Yet I want to draw your attention to a greater nobility. One which is a gift indeed. You see, when we gave our lives to Christ, God made us royalty. Scripture states that we are "A CHOSEN RACE, A royal PRIESTHOOD, A HOLY NATION, A PEOPLE FOR God's OWN POSSESSION, so that you may proclaim the excellencies of Him who has called you out of darkness into His marvelous light." 1 Peter 2:9

In another place we are told that "He has made us to be a kingdom, priests to His God and Father." This adoption into God's family had made us partakers of His Royalty. You are royalty. You have a place at God's table.

Without Blemish

The second gift that Nebuchadnezzar was looking for in these young men was that they be "impeccable" or "without blemish." In this day people with disabilities were considered anathema. Nebuchadnezzer did not want anyone with a disability in his royal court. Thank God that we have come a long way in society from that backwards way of thinking.

Today we recognize at least in our informed society, disabilities are not character flaws. But I'd like to pose a question. Do you know anyone who doesn't have some kind of disability? I think the honest answer is no. In fact I'm quite sure that we are all imperfect. I've met people with great athleticism who struggle with dyslexia. I've met incredibly brilliant people who struggle with irrational fears. I think we are all a little crazy, and that makes us human.

The fact is we are all fallen creatures, born with not enough or sometimes too much of something. The difference is some of us have a disability which can be covered up more easily than others. I like to think that our limitations are a key to our destiny and ought to be explored.

But again, let's look at this in a deeper way. There really is no such thing as a perfect person. There really isn't anyone who is "without blemish." Or it there? The fact is that if you are in Christ, forgiven of your sin He has rendered you blameless.

Excellent Quality of Appearance

This one is kind of funny when you think about it. Nebuchadnezzar wanted "good looking men" in his court. It's funny because it's so subjective. The fact is that really the original text implies that these men had to have excellent quality of appearance. They needed to carry themselves with confidence, and dignity. They weren't sloppy or slobs. Excellence defined these men. This is still a value in our day and ought to be considered by anyone seeking to have influence for the Kingdom of God. The simple fact is that honor is never inappropriate. And when a person dresses and carries themselves in a way that honors the environment they are in, it is a winning strategy.

I recall one occasion where I was invited to speak at a youth event in Houston. I made the mistake of not asking what the protocol was for the event. I arrived in a suit and tie, for what turned out to be an outreach to "heavy metal rock" enthusiasts. In that scenario I was dishonoring the protocol by being dressed in a way that was un-relatable to the audience. Big mistake, but lesson learned.

In another cases I have seen a speaker arrive underdressed for an event where everyone was in professional business attire. The speaker felt very comfortable, but almost no one took him seriously. So here is a basic tip. Know your "palace" and dress accordingly. But dress at the highest level for that environment. In a way that demonstrates that you honor them and the God you represent.

What's always been funny to me is that when David faced Goliath, David's good looks were one on his criticism. Scriptures says that the Philistine distained David because he was "young, ruddy, and good looking." If your enemies are going to criticize you, and with will. Let it be because you have an excellent quality of appearance.

Teachability

Thus far we have seen how at times we will be called to go places where the standards are higher than that to which we are accustomed. In this situation you should not see higher standards as an obstacle, but rather an opportunity. When you are given an opportunity to step up and develop yourself. Take it! And watch God help you grow, and use you for his sake. Notice the final three qualifications for service in this elite group, an "intelligence in every branch of wisdom, endowment with understanding, and discerning knowledge."[87] To say it simply they must be teachable. No matter what doors open, or how high a man may go he must always remain teachable. This is the surest route to promotion.

A teachable spirit is a value to you and those you serve. The absence of one costs everyone. Think about the people in your life who have accomplished the most. I guarantee you that teachabilty is an attribute of their life. When God gave Solomon a blank check and told him to ask for anything he wanted. Solomon replied "Give Your servant an understanding heart to judge Your people to discern between good and evil. For who is able to judge this great people of Yours?" 1 Kings 3:9

He basically said "Lord, make me teachable." And God not only gave him wisdom, but honor, wealth, influence, and power as well.

Solomon later wrote:

Whoever loves discipline loves knowledge, But he who hates reproof is stupid. Proverbs 12:1

Take my instruction and not silver, And knowledge rather than choicest gold. Proverbs 8:10

Take hold of instruction; do not let go. Guard her, for she is your life. Prov 4:13

Give instruction to a wise man and he will be still wiser, Teach a   righteous man and he will increase his learning. Proverbs 9:9

He is on the path of life who heeds instruction, But he who ignores reproof goes astray. Proverbs 10:17

---

[87] Daniel 1:4

A poor yet wise lad is better than an old and foolish king who no longer knows how to receive instruction.   Eccl 4:13

Are you teachable? Do you love instruction? Do you value instruction more than silver? The answer to that question will not only determine how far you get in life, but also whether or not you receive the Favor of God. We came into this world ignorant; only instruction can change that.

Teach-ability is a choice we must make and a lifestyle we must adopt intentionally.   And the fact is that living in the information age has eradicated all excuses for ignorance. We have at our disposal knowledge unparalleled in human experience. At rates of speed that are astounding. Yet there must be a thirst for knowledge, cultivated and pursued. So let me ask a few questions that might help you figure out whether you are teachable or not.

1.   Do you find yourself being argumentative when you receive correction or a critique?

The proverb says "correct a fool and he will hate you, correct a wise man and he will love you." I have found that even my most off based critics can teach me something worth learning. Maybe I don't agree with their assessment, or enjoy their criticism. But there is always a take away which might benefit me and the people I serve. If they are right, then I can address the problem. If they are wrong, then I can address the reason for the misperception. But in every case there is an opportunity to learn. I bet most of the correction you will receive in your life is actually not coming from malice. So rather than be argumentative, listen to what's being said and look for the lesson.

2.   Do you shift blame for your failures to others?

When we shift blame to others, we assume that we could not have done things better or differently. The refusal to accept our responsibility closes to the door to learning. This is a big sign that you are not teachable.

3.   Do you surround yourself with "yes" men?

If you have surrounded yourself with "yes" men it's most

likely because you don't want to hear another opinion. If no one can tell you no, or that you're wrong, you will never be able to grow. Maintaining open channels of honest input is vital to any growth. But it is essential in leadership whether in the home, the church, or the marketplace.

In an article in the Harvard Business Review Noreena Hertz writes "When group members are actively encouraged to openly express divergent opinions, they not only share more information, they consider it more systematically and in a more balanced and less biased way. When people engage with those with different opinions and views from their own they become much more capable of properly interrogating critical assumptions and identifying creative alternatives." If everyone in your sphere of influence is reasserting the same ideas, you may find yourself walking in circles, or worse yet, the wrong circle.

Let me sum it up with a Jeff Foxworthy-type summation. If you don't read, take notes, ask questions or listen, you might be unteachable.

Barriers to Teachability

The lack of a teachable spirit generally comes from the root of pride, insecurity, and even apathy.

Pride

Pride leads you to believe that you already know everything. It blinds you to the fact that we don't know everything, and can't know everything. Scriptures states that "pride goes before the fall." And the book of James tell us the God "resist the proud, but gives favor to the humble." Pride can weaken the strongest of men and render useless many a gifted man.

Insecurity

Insecurity is another root cause. Because insecurity leads us to believe that we can't afford to let anyone know that we don't know. Yet if you think about it, this is the greatest way to stay in the dark. In my experience with teaching, the question that one person asks is often the question that others wanted to ask but wouldn't. Insecurity is pride behind a veil of humility. This is false humility.

Apathy

Apathy is the most common of the roots in this century. The general laziness of assuming that we already know enough is pervasive in our culture. Proverb says "The sluggard is wiser in his own eyes than seven men who can give a discreet answer." (Proverbs 26:16) I don't think this in intentional, but most apathy isn't. It's just a passive attitude towards growth and progress that reduces many to fruitlessness.

God's Standards

As we have seen, Daniel was willing to honor the standards of the palace and as a result was placed in high places. But that is not the whole story. The fact is that Daniel not only honored the King's standards, but more importantly, he honored Gods standards. This is where Favor really takes off. If honoring an earthy king can bring a man favor, how much more will the fear of the Lord?

Proverbs 15:16 says "In the light of a king's face is life, And his favor is like a cloud with the spring rain." Daniel knew that he had more to lose by dishonoring God, than any dishonor of Nebuchadnezzar.

Part of the preparation for serving the king was eating a Babylonian diet. This included food that was not kosher, and forbidden by the Law of God. Daniel "made up his mind that he would not defile himself with the kings choice food or with the wine which he drank."

As a result, he sought permission from his commander to abstain from eating the provided meals. Thus far Daniel had submitted to the entire process. But breaking his Jewish diet would not be entertained. He had been brought up from birth to honor the Law of God. Now his faith was being put to the test. The adage goes "When in Rome, do as the Romans." But not for Daniel, though in Babylon he would not do as the Babylonians.

A 21st Century Christian mind can hardly imagine such a conflict. This seems like an easy choice. Eat the food, don't rock the boat. But Daniel understood the anatomy of compromise. Small compromises always lead to great ones. Daniel decided rather to fear God than men. As a result, the scripture states that "God granted Daniel Favor and compassion in the sight of the commander of the official." Indeed "none of those who wait on the Lord will ever be put to shame."

Now that Daniel had favor in the sight of his commander, he used the opportunity to glorify God. The commander was afraid that if Daniel and his fellows didn't eat the king's rations, they would grow weak and sick. He said if this happens "I will be forfeiting my head."

Daniel said, "Test your servants for ten days, and let us be given some vegetables to eat and water to drink. Then you decide what to do with us." Daniel did a colossal trust fall into the arms of God.

As he made the arrangement with the commander, he was actually thrusting himself onto the God he feared. He had no idea that this small moment of faith would be the predecessor to major tests of faith to come. After the ten day test Daniel and his fellows were healthier, and more robust that all the others in the program. The honored the king and they honored God, in turn they found that the favor of God rested on them.

Chapter 7

The Coat of Blood

So they took Joseph's tunic, and slaughtered a male goat and dipped the tunic in the blood; 32 and they sent the varicolored tunic and brought it to their father and said, "We found this; please examine it to see whether it is your son's tunic or not." 33 Then he examined it and said, "It is my son's tunic. A wild beast has devoured him; Joseph has surely been torn to pieces!" Genesis 37:31-32

After selling Joseph to the traveling merchants, the brothers now had a new problem on their hands. They must explain Joseph's disappearance to their father. The clever sons of Jacob hatched a perfect plot. They took a lamb from the flock and slaughtered it. They then took the blood of that lamb and smeared it over Joseph's coat of many colors. They then took that coat to Jacob and Jacob surmised that His son was torn apart by a wild beast. The plot worked so well that it would have surprised even them. But in carrying it out, they stumbled upon the great truth of the atonement.

Joseph went away a slave but alive, and a lamb had to die in his place. This prefigured the ultimate substitution of all believers. At the Cross the Lamb of God would be offered that the believer might go free. Furthermore, this event pointed to another fact. The brothers figured that blood would be a perfect cover for their sin. And indeed it was. For you see, only blood can cover sin. For them it bought time, and eventually salvation from famine. For us, the blood of Christ purchased innumerable benefits, among them salvation from sin. The writer of Hebrews said "Without the shedding of blood there is no remission for sin." These men inadvertently stumbled upon the greatest truth of the Gospel and proclaimed through their treachery a coming day of atonement.

Joseph's Coat of many colors now takes on yet another meaning. In the first place we see the Favor of God the Father, but now we see the work of Christ the Son in the Atonement. This is not the first time such a type is seen in scripture, nor is it the only. In fact the Old Testament is replete with types and shadows of the blood of Christ. In fact there in no doctrine of scripture more clearly taught from Genesis to Revelation than that of the Blood.

The First Shedding of Blood

From the opening pages of Human history, we find a marvelous reference to the blood. Adam and Eve had fallen into sin, and the whole race of men with them. With their eyes now open by sin, they saw that they were naked and sough to cover their sin. They took fig leaves and made coverings for shame. When the Lord came into the Garden He found them covered.

Then we see the very first type of the atonement in Bible history. The Lord takes an animal, which I believe to have been a lamb and slaughtered it for clothing. This is the very first time that blood was shed in the history of the world and it was for the covering of sin.

The Passover

The scope of progressive revelation continued to broaden as we enter into the book of Exodus. Again the blood is seen in dramatic fashion as the instrument of salvation. On the night of the Passover the Lord instructed Israel to slaughter a lamb per household. The blood of that Lamb was then to be taken and applied to the door post of their home. That night the angel of death passed over the land of Egypt. Any home that did not have blood on its door post would suffer the loss of its first born among men or beast.

And so it was that in the house of the Egyptians there was heard the weeping, sorrow and lament of mourning. But in the household of those who applied the blood there was heard the sound of joy and peace. It's as if as the angel of death passed over Egypt the blood on the door post would announce "Death has already been here, you cannot stop here." This is the very kernel of Gospel truth. The blood of Christ has covered the believer, and over our heart is written to wrath and judgment "death has already been here."

The Feast of Atonement

In Leviticus we see the widening of revelation yet again. This time the blood would extend beyond a man of a household, to a nation. In a series of seven Feasts, the Lord drew Israel annually to himself. Towards the culmination of festal year was the Great Day of Atonement. The sixth feast offered the broadest picture of the influence of the blood.

Unlike the other feasts, this was not a feast of Joy, it was a time for the "affliction of the soul." Dr. Kellogg has stated that the portions of Scripture regarding the Atonement are the "most significant portions of the law of God." The word "Atonement" in Hebrew means "to cover. Thus, on the great day of Atonement the sins of the people would be covered from the sight of God, for one year.

It is interesting to note that the word "Atonement" in the New Testament no longer simply means "to cover," now it literally means "to take away." Christ in the Atonement at the cross did not merely cover our sin, but he forever removed it from the sight of God.

On the Great Day of Atonement the High Priest was alone in the Tabernacle. No one else was allowed to participate or observe the ritual. This particularity speaks volumes when we view the

Cross, for it was there where God alone worked out man's redemption, and in the dark of Calvary no one would witness the sight. Lev. 16:17

Beyond entering alone, the High Priest also dressed differently for this feast. The High Priest was generally dressed with robes of majesty and splendor. Bright colors depicting his royal status in the service of God, were normal attire. Yet on the day of atonement, he would lay aside his robes of splendor. He would enter into the Tabernacle wearing a simple white tunic. This act though veiled in its meaning for thousands of years, pointed to the humiliation of Christ.

Our great heavenly high priest laid aside the robes of majesty. He left behind the ivory palaces of heaven. He dressed in the humble tunic of human flesh, and offered atonement for our sins. Just as Joseph was stripped of his coat to comply with the demands of his brothers, so to was Christ. Yet no one stripped him of his majesty, except he himself laid it down.

On the Day of Atonement there were a Sin Offering, and a Burnt offering. The Burnt Offering consisted of a Ram, which was offered up in a whole burnt offering to the Lord. The Sin Offering that was offered on the day of Atonement, was a pair of Goats. The Priest would cast a lot to determine which goat would live and which one would die. The Goat which lived was called the Scapegoat and the goat that died was the "Lords." Lev. 16:7-14

The goat which was chosen to die was offered as a Sin Offering before the Lord. Then Moses would place his hand upon the Scapegoat and release it into the Wilderness. What a marvelous picture of Christ and His Church. He became our Sin Offering, and bore our sin in His own body, while we were allowed to go free.

The great Day of Atonement was the only day of the year where the High Priest would enter beyond the veil into the Holy of Holies. (Lev 16:34, Heb. 9:7) On this day he would enter twice, once with the blood of a bullock which was for the Atonement of his own sins, and then again with the blood of the Goat which was Atonement for the Sins of the Nation.

The All Effective Blood of Christ

Christ entered into the Holy of Holies, not with the blood of bulls and goats, but with His own blood, once and for all. J.I. Packer, in his classic *Knowing God*, asks the question: "Has the word propitiation any place in your Christianity? It does, whether we know it or not. At the heart of the work of Christ is the sacrifice in His blood, which the Bible states that God put forth as a propitiation for our sins." Few other doctrines go to the heart of the Christian faith like the Atonement. Congregations sing at the top of their lungs: "My sin, not in part but the whole, has been nailed to the cross, so I bear it no more, praise the Lord, praise the Lord, O my soul!" ("It Is Well with My Soul"). The priestly work of Christ separates Christianity from Judaism and Islam. Not surprisingly, the Cross has become the symbol for our faith."[88]

At its core, the Coat of our Father gave us is a Coat of Blood. The centrality of the Gospel to our purpose is indisputable. When evangelist John Wesley (1703-1791) was returning home from a service one night, he was robbed. The thief, however, found his victim to have only a little money and some Christian literature. As the bandit was leaving, Wesley called out, "Stop! I have something more to give you." The surprised robber paused. "My friend," said Wesley, "you may live to regret this sort of life. If you ever do, here's something to remember: 'The blood of Jesus Christ cleanses us from all sin!'" The thief hurried away, and Wesley prayed that his words might bear fruit.

Years later, Wesley was greeting people after a Sunday service when he was approached by a stranger. What a surprise to learn that this visitor, now a believer in Christ as a successful businessman, was the one who had robbed him years before! "I owe it all to you," said the transformed man. "Oh no, my friend," Wesley exclaimed, "not to me, but to the precious blood of Christ that cleanses us from all sin!"

It is at the cross where we see love on display in its most remarkable way. Love not feint or faked. Love not forged or forced. But love simple and free. Love running in red from the

---

[88] Mark Dever Article, Nothing But The Blood.

rich wounds of the Messiah. "The world takes us to a silver screen on which flickering images of passion and romance play, and as we watch, the world says, "This is love." God takes us to the foot of a tree on which a naked and bloodied man hangs and says, "This is love."[89]

It is the blood that grants the believer access to the presence of a holy God and peace in the passing from this life to the next. Spurgeon preached it saying "In the last dread hour of death, when conscience looks at sin as it really is and no longer is blinded, nothing can bring it peace but the blood of the Lamb! Nothing can give the soul repose when it is about to meet its God, except the knowledge that Christ was made a curse for us that we might be blessed in Him[90]

Note with me from the scriptures what the results of the blood of Christ are in the life of the believer.

Propitiation through His Blood

"But now apart from the Law the righteousness of God has been manifested, being witnessed by the Law and the Prophets, even the righteousness of God through faith in Jesus Christ for all those who believe; for there is no distinction; for all have sinned and fall short of the glory of God, being justified as a gift by His grace through the redemption which is in Christ Jesus; whom God displayed publicly as a propitiation in His blood through faith. This was to demonstrate His righteousness, because in the forbearance of God He passed over the sins previously committed; for the demonstration, I say, of His righteousness at the present time, so that He would be just and the justifier of the one who has faith in Jesus." Romans 3:21-26

Redemption through His Blood

"In Him we have redemption through His blood, the forgiveness of our trespasses, according to the riches of His grace." Ephesians 1:7

---

[89] Joshua Harris, *I Kissed Dating Goodbye: A New Attitude Toward Relationships and Romance*
[90] Spurgeon, Charles. Sermon #2839

Cleansing through His Blood

1 John 1:7 "If we say that we have fellowship with Him and *yet* walk in the darkness, we lie and do not practice the truth; but if we walk in the Light as He Himself is in the Light, we have fellowship with one another, and the blood of Jesus His Son cleanses us from all sin.

Justification through His Blood

Much more then, having now been justified by His blood, we shall be saved from the wrath of God through Him. Romans 5:9

Communion with God through the Blood

Is not the cup of blessing which we bless a sharing in the blood of Christ? Is not the bread which we break a sharing in the body of Christ? 1 Corinthians 10:16

New Covenant in His Blood

For this is My blood of the covenant, which is poured out for many for forgiveness of sins. Matthew 26:28

Drawn near to God by the Blood

But now in Christ Jesus you who formerly were far off have been brought near by the blood of Christ. Ephesians 2:13

Peace through is Blood

For it was the Father's good pleasure for all the fullness to dwell in Him, and through Him to reconcile all things to Himself, having made peace through the blood of His cross; through Him, I say, whether things on earth or things in heaven. Col 1:19-20

Remission of Sins through His Blood

And according to the Law, one may almost say, all things are cleansed with blood, and without shedding of blood there is no forgiveness. Hebrews 9:22

Access to Gods Holy presence through His Blood

Therefore, brethren, since we have confidence to enter the holy place by the blood of Jesus, by a new and living way which He inaugurated for us through the veil, that is, His flesh, and since we have a great priest over the house of God, let us draw near with a sincere heart in full assurance of faith, having our hearts sprinkled clean from an evil conscience and our bodies washed with pure water. Hebrews 10:19-22

The cleansing of the Conscience through the Blood

For if the blood of goats and bulls and the ashes of a heifer sprinkling those who have been defiled sanctify for the cleansing of the flesh, 14how much more will the blood of Christ, who through the eternal Spirit offered Himself without blemish to God, cleanse your conscience from dead works to serve the living God? Hebrews 9:13-14

We will know by this that we are of the truth, and will assure our heart before Him in whatever our heart condemns us; for God is greater than our heart and knows all things. Beloved, if our heart does not condemn us, we have confidence before God; and whatever we ask we receive from Him, because we keep His commandments and do the things that are pleasing in His sight. 1 John 3:19-22

Preaching the Blood of the Cross

What are we to do with this message? Are we to discard it as old fashioned as some have? Are we to avoid mention of the blood in our witness lest it offend the sensitivities of the culture? No, may it never be. We must be about the business of preaching the only message which saves sinners and makes them right before God. We must preach the blood for in it alone is sins payment made in full. Through it man averts the wrath of God justly due his sin. No other message can accomplish this, only the cross of Christ can do that.

Some years ago, a well know department store found its self in need of a new approach. The Sears name had become synonymous with tools, fire grills, and big screen TV's. Its sales were down, and they decided to try a new approach. In ads most can recall, they pitched a new slogan, "The Softer Side of Sears." In short it reflected the fact that the store had many items which "women" would enjoy. They not only sold tools, but linens, pillows, clothing, and fine china. Weather the approach worked or not is unknown to this author, but it seems to have been adopted by a modern segment of the church today.

Many behind the pulpit in our generation have taken a softer approach to the Bible. Assuming that it will in turn render the sweet reward of larger numbers on Sunday morning and greater profits at the book store. Were it not that eternal souls are hanging in the balance, one could merely dismiss the "new approach" as a cleaver tactic. However at the center of this softer message is a sinister attack on the "Cross of Christ." They have begun to preach a softer side of the cross, a message which I submit is not the Gospel at all. Some refuse to make mention of the blood or even the cross in their sermons.

In Galatians chapter five, the apostle Paul states "and I brethren, if I yet preach circumcision why do I yet suffer persecution? Then the offense of the cross ceased."[91] In this text we do not see Paul condemning the offensive nature of the cross, but rather defending its offense. In the Greek text we find the word "scandal" in place of the word offence, which communicated the fact that the preaching of the cross is intended to stir conflict in the hearts of men.

We also find the term in the first chapter of 1 Corinthians in which the same apostle states, "For indeed the Jews require a sign and Greeks search for wisdom; but we preach Christ crucified, to Jews a stumbling block (scandal) and to Gentiles foolishness..."[92] The use of the term in both passages indicates an inherent offensiveness to the preaching of the Cross." While the Cross is the message of Gods mercy and love toward man, it carries in its self a matter which disgusts every man. To preach laws, and rituals was not at all offensive to a man's conscience, but to

---

[91] Galatians 5:11
[92] 1 Corinthians 1:23

suggest that simple faith in a slain lamb, could save, is offensive to the prideful mind of men.

This fact should not surprise anyone. The Prophet Isaiah states "He has no stately majesty that we should look upon him, nor appearance that we should be attracted to Him." His Passion at Calvary was the worst fate any man could suffer, and the wrath of God which fell upon Him was fearsome to behold. It's acceptable to preach redemption through any other means, but please don't lay the fate of all humanity at the feet of this unbecoming image of dead man. While it may be common to find such a view from the outside of the church, it is painful to see a generation from the inside which holds the view that the offense of the Cross must be softened in order to appeal to the masses.

The primary reason for this offense is that it directly reveals the sinful nature of man. The cross is by design the great "whistle blower." It boldly and un-apologetically screams that man is guilty of sin. Were sin not the problem, the cross would not have been the solution. But sin is the problem. It seems mankind is all too comfortable with sin, so long as it's not addressed as such.

The philosopher calls it evil, the media calls it a mistake, and no one seems offended. But when a preacher calls it sin, offense is never far behind. The reason for this, is that the cross lays the cause for God's wrath squarely at the feet of the individual. We have become a culture where the serial killer is a victim of his poor upbringing, and the drunk is the unwitting casualty of external conditions out of his control. No one is reasonable for their own sins; it's always someone else's fault.

On the cross we see image of Gods perfect son, hanging in shameful display. Receiving in His own body the wrath of a Holy God for sins committed by every man, woman, and child, since Adam. We see him paying the penalty of a broken law, which He alone preserved unbroken. We see his bleeding side and wounded hands, as proof of payment, the receipt for sin. Bearing in His own soul, the horrible atrocities of genocide, abortion, rape, adultery, fornication, child molestation, theft, bribery, injustice, and murder, compounded by the inoffensive little sins such as white lies, lust, hate, grudges, forgiveness, mercilessness, excess, gluttony, in chastity, and innocent personal private pride.

Just exactly who was it that committed all of those crimes against a Holy God, if in fact it's someone else's fault. For whom was this billed played, and in whose name did this invoice of unrighteousness arrive. Surely someone was at fault, someone was guilty, someone culpable, responsible, condemnable. That someone was me! It is I to whom the stroke was due. I am guilty, culpable, responsible, and condemnable. His rejection by His own Father, His crushing for sin, His bruise, and His stripes, are all my fault. We look at the bloody broken body of Gods perfect son, and our hearts must cry "I did that to Him."

This is why the Cross is such a scandal, because it points to man's sinful nature as the sum and cause of Christ's sacrifice at the Cross. For anyone to attempt to soften that reality is an assault on the very purpose for which Christ died. If God did not soften the cross for His own son, why should any preacher soften the message for any wicked and undeserving sinner? How can one truly understand the work of Grace, if he does not first understand the weight of sinful guilt? The cross is not a band aid on a boo-boo, it the full scale exhumation of man's dead, sinful, soul from sin.

In response to this eternal truth, sinful humanity is called to repent for sin. At the core of that repentance must be an understanding that we are guilty as charged. If the preacher or layman choose to soften that reality, he does more to harm the Kingdom of God, than the perpetrators of false religions around the globe. For in claiming to preach Christ, they are actually not preaching at all. To remove the Cross from Christ is to remove the very purpose for which he became the incarnate Son of God. The preacher and layman alike must affirm with Paul, "we preach Christ Crucified."[93] "For the word of the cross is foolishness to those who are perishing, but to us who are being saved it is the power of God.[94]

Singing About The Blood

One of the richest traditions of worship inherited from the

---

[93] 1 Corinthians 1:23
[94] 1 Corinthians 1:18

American Awakenings was hymns about the blood of Christ. I love modern worship styles and rejoice in the worship movements of the last two decades. But I fear that these movements have inadvertently left out of 21st Century worship songs some vital elements of theology. Sacred music's purpose has always been to inform our faith, as well as inspire our faith.

Much of modern worship succeeds in inspiration but fails to teach doctrine. I was born into the last score of years of the 20th Century. So I can mark a clear difference in my mind from the worship of my childhood and that of my college and young adulthood. Styles have changed and that is a good thing. The church should always be in the lead in cultural revolutions of style and expression. But the doctrine of the church has suffered in the process.

We too rarely hear songs written today that call our attention to heaven, consecration, or the blood of Jesus. I think we have lost our view of eternity or heaven and hence make little of it in singing. The temporal concerns of our day have outweighed our eternal nature. This has had consequences which are devastating to personal holiness, corporate commitment, and great commission urgency. A few months ago I started leading my congregation in singing old consecration hymns. As we did this I realized that in contrast to the new songs which I love, there is a great difference. Today's worship songs seldom call us to consecration, surrender, or sacrifice. This too, no doubt with devastating consequences.

Now, to the issue at hand. We have stopped singing about the blood. This I'm quite sure has been intentional for some. And for those who simply flow with the currents of popularity, the result is accidental but costly. Some time ago the seeker sensitive movement waged a subtle war on the blood. They assumed that in order to appeal to "seekers" (that is newcomers), you had to leave out references to the blood. I guess modern sensitivities can't handle references to bleeding lambs and a dying savior. This is odd considering that some modern pulpits are filled with "cussing preachers" and sexually explicit sermon content. Have we become put off by the blood of Jesus, and lured by vulgarity in the pulpit? Surly this is nothing less than satanic deception.

With that said, I urge you, whether pastor, music minister, elder, or congregant, to insist upon the inclusion of such lyrics regardless of style which set before the hearts of your people the sacred truth of the blood. This truth must never be far from our singing, so that the essence of the Gospel may never be far from our hearts.

A bloodless church has no power, and that is far too convenient for the sworn enemy of our souls. Consider that when we get to heaven, we will still be singing about the blood of the Lamb. Even then our savior's blood will remain the subject of our songs. If it is so in heaven, where sin no longer reigns, and Satan no longer deceives. Then all the more, let us proclaim salvation through Christ blood while pilgrims on this earth.

And they sang a new song, saying, Worthy are You to take the book and to break its seals; for You were slain, and purchased for God with Your blood men from every tribe and tongue and people and nation. Revelation 5:9

Chapter 8

The Anointing

Now there are varieties of gifts, but the same Spirit. And there are varieties of ministries, and the same Lord. There are varieties of effects, but the same God who works all things in all persons. 1 Corinthians 12:4-6

We have seen the powerful influence of the Favor of God, and the Blood of Christ in the coat our Father has given us. Now we turn our attention to the third and final aspect of the coat. The Father's Favor, the Son's atonement, and now the Spirit's Anointing. Scripture states that Joseph was given a coat of many colors. I submit to you that within the diversity of the colors we see a type of the Holy Spirit.

The bible described the manifestation of the Holy Spirit as being a "varieties of gifts, but the same Spirit, and varieties of service, and the same Lord. Varieties of effects, but the same God who works all things in all persons."[95] This diversity is native to the work of God, because God is infinite in his creativity. He has not made us in a cookie cutter way, fitting into forms and functions. Rather, He has made us a unique expression of His divine life, and given us the gifts needed to manifest His glory in

---

[95] 1 Corinthians 12:4-6

our days. Note the three categories of this diversity; variety of gifts, variety of service, and variety of effects.

Gifts

First we note that God has given a plurality of gifts. This word gift is the Greek word "charisma" from which we derive the term charismatic. Its modern usage of the word charismatic is interesting because we understand it to mean someone who is compelling and inspiring. But the original use of the word "charisma" is most important, because it literally means "a gift of divine grace." In other words your spiritual gift is actually a grace gift given as an act of divine favor, for the accomplishing of divine goals. The gifts of God are as diverse as the purposes of God in each individual life. To each person God has given a divine assignment, as well as the gifts to fulfill it.

Consider Joseph. He was gifted with administrative capacities which lead to the saving of Egypt's economy during a seven-year famine. He was gifted with discernment, word of wisdom, and word of Knowledge. Each of which brought him closer to his God-desired purpose. At no point in his life did Joseph ever require a gift which he did not have in his arsenal. And so it shall be with you.

Another implication which we should derive from this it that "grace gifts" actually have a dual flow of grace. On the one hand when you received the gift, it came as a gracious act of God's choice. Functioning in that gift produces the reward of usefulness and that is indeed a "gift of grace." On the other hand, when you function in your gift, it becomes grace to someone else. Your function of the gift becomes a conduit by which you become a blessing to others. Conversely, when you sit on your gift, you stifle the flow of that blessing to others.

I ask you a pointed question on this front. "How many people are waiting for your gift to be activated?" Often when we go through trials, or difficulties we turn inward, and stop functioning in our gifts. While we shut off the flow of that anointing, we also block an avenue through which God can strengthen us in the trail. You will find that if you will serve someone else even in your trials, God will see to it that your need gets met.

When we talk about gifts we should keep in mind the following five truths:

1. Every believer has a Spiritual Gift.
2. The Gifts were given to build up the Body of Christ.
3. These Gifts are permanent.
4. The believer is expected to use their Gifts.
5. The Gifts need to be discovered and perfected.

Let's unpack each of these truth and make application to our lives.

1. Every believer has a Spiritual Gift.

Scripture states that the Holy Spirit works all these things *"distributing to each one individually just as He wills.*[96] He distributes to each one, which means you. No one is left without a gift. You may not have received the same gifts I received, but we have all received gifts as an act of Gods sovereign will, for the purpose and design of his making. Therefor we do well not to covet someone else's gift. Because they were given these gifts for the accomplishing of a divine agenda, which most likely is very different from yours.

I struggled with this for a while. I grew up in the era of R.W. Schambach and heard of the great exploits of A.A. Allen and Smith Wigglesworth. These guys raised the dead, and healed the sick in their sleep! Well not quite, but that how it seemed to me. I wanted so much to be like them. My gifts in ministry were less demonstrative as it turned out. Although I have operated in the gifts of healing on occasion, I own that that was not my primary gift.

When I was a boy my father's fractured jaw was healed after I prayed for him in a prayer line in Bloomington, Texas. I must have been about 10-years old and I was preaching a three-day revival. Though he never told me personally (probable so that I would not get a swelled head), I overheard him tell my grandmother how his jaw had been healed in that service. She said "Perhaps he will

---

[96] 1 Corinthians 12:11

operate in the gift of healing." I wish now that he had spoken to me about it, perhaps it would have stimulated a greater faith in my heart towards that gift.

On another occasion, a woman testified concerning my preaching as a boy in one of my Uncle's Revival Tents. She said "I thought for sure that little boy was being told what to say. I figured there was an ear piece in his ear, and they were telling him what to say! But then he prayed with me for healing, and I was healed."

As I grew older, these things spurred a great ambition within me for the gifts of healing. Oh how I wanted to see the sick healed and I did from time to time. I have seen numerous people healed, but I never was used quite like those men I mentioned before.

No, it seemed God had other ways he wanted to use me, gifts which would be better suited to the purpose he had given me in my life. I believe that I operate in the Preaching Gift which the Bible calls Prophecy. This gift was mine from childhood and I consider it the greatest treasure of my life. Sometimes it's as if I'm standing outside of myself and watching as the Holy Spirit brings forth His word through me.

I also believe that the Lord has given me the gift of government or leadership which the Bible calls "administration." Again, from childhood, I have observed how the Lord has granted me various leadership offices, and he does so even now. If people were to stand in line for spiritual gifts, the cue would be miles long for miracles and healing. But not too many people would sign up for "government." What a boring gift! Who needs it! I myself did not recognize its presence within me, nor its value in general until life and experience had granted me a little insight into its importance. But it seems so precious to me now, in light of God's assignments and program for my life.

All of this to say, that you may not have the gifts you covet in others, but you have the gifts you need. And every believer can count on the perfect and sovereign work of the Holy Spirit in distributing to each the gifts needed to fulfill their assignment.

2. The Gifts were given to build up the Body of Christ.

No gift was ever given for the personal private use or benefit of the recipient. Rather they were given for the benefit of the Body of Christ as a whole. "And He gave some as apostles, and some as prophets, and some as evangelists, and some as pastors and teachers, for the equipping of the saints for the work of service, to the building up of the body of Christ; until we all attain to the unity of the faith, and of the knowledge of the Son of God, to a mature man, to the measure of the stature which belongs to the fullness of Christ."[97] We notice here that the fivefold ministry was given to "equip the saints, and for edifying the body." No one is an Apostle for his own sake, or a prophet for his own good. No one ever serves as Pastor for his own benefit, but rather for the service of others. Furthermore we are told in 1 Corinthians 12:7 that "each one is given the manifestation of the Spirit for the common good." In other words when you operate in your spiritual gift it will be expedient for everyone, and profitable to all. "That's a result of the manifestation of God the Spirit in the life of the church—good comes to people. It is good for people to see God. It is good for us to see the manifestations of God's Spirit in each other's lives."[98]

3. These Gifts are permanent.

While this truth may be hard to swallow for some, the scripture states that "for the gifts and the calling of God are irrevocable."[99] This means that God does not take back the gifts he give the believer. Sin without a doubt will hinder the use and operation of the gifts. Causing them to lie dormant until such time as repentance has entered that heart. God has not changed his mind concerning the fallen believer, and desires above all that they may be retorted to the full use of those gifts. The gifts themselves remain yours, and are yours to use according to the measure of faith you are willing to exercise. Peter denied Christ three times and yet was restored not only to fellowship but was also greatly anointed to preach on the day of Pentecost. I am convinced that Judas himself could have been restored if he had repented. There is not depth to great for the grace of God to reach.

---

[97] Ephesians 4:11-13
[98] JohnPiper. "Living in the Spirit and in the Body for the Common Good." Desiring God. N.p., 29 Nov. 1992. Web.
[99] Romans 11:29

And anyone who will repent will find that the gifts are his to function in for the glory of God.

4. The believer is expected to use their Gifts.

The Apostle Peter admonishes us saying "As each one has received a special gift, employ it in serving one another as good stewards of the manifold grace of God."[100] First he makes the point we have already seen above, that "everyone has a gift." Then he charges us to "employ" that gift. To employ is to use the gifts given to serve others. No gift is ever given so that it can sit on a shelf unused and unfruitful.

Jesus told a parable that make this point very clear. He said:

"For it is just like a man about to go on a journey, who called his own slaves and entrusted his possessions to them. To one he gave five talents, to another, two, and to another, one, each according to his own ability; and he went on his journey. Immediately the one who had received the five talents went and traded with them, and gained five more talents. In the same manner the one who had received the two talents gained two more. But he who received the one talent went away, and dug a hole in the ground and hid his master's money.

"Now after a long time the master of those slaves came and settled accounts with them. The one who had received the five talents came up and brought five more talents, saying, 'Master, you entrusted five talents to me. See, I have gained five more talents.' His master said to him, 'Well done, good and faithful slave. You were faithful with a few things, I will put you in charge of many things; enter into the joy of your master.'

"Also the one who had received the two talents came up and said, 'Master, you entrusted two talents to me. See, I have gained two more talents.' His master said to him, 'Well done, good and faithful slave. You were faithful with a few things, I will put you in charge of many things; enter into the joy of your master.'

---

[100] 1 Peter 4:10

"And the one also who had received the one talent came up and said, 'Master, I knew you to be a hard man, reaping where you did not sow and gathering where you scattered no seed. 'And I was afraid, and went away and hid your talent in the ground. See, you have what is yours.'

"But his master answered and said to him, 'You wicked, lazy slave, you knew that I reap where I did not sow and gather where I scattered no seed. 'Then you ought to have put my money in the bank, and on my arrival I would have received my money back with interest. 'Therefore take away the talent from him, and give it to the one who has the ten talents.'

"For to everyone who has, more shall be given, and he will have an abundance; but from the one who does not have, even what he does have, shall be taken away. "Throw out the worthless slave into the outer darkness; in that place there will be weeping and gnashing of teeth."[101]

We can draw from this Parable the following truths.

First of all, we see that God expects a return on the gifts he's given men. In the fifteenth chapter of John we see that God demands fruit, good fruit, and much fruit from his children.[102] In Matthew twenty-one we see that Jesus cursed the fig tree for its fruitlessness.[103] And in this parable of the talents we see the principle again. The Master is going to return someday to settle accounts, and he will reward those who have produced some fruit on the gifts they were given. Not everyone receives the same gifts, but everyone is expected to bear fruit from the gifts they have received.

Peter writes "Now for this very reason also, applying all diligence, in your faith supply moral excellence, and in your moral excellence, knowledge, and in your knowledge, self-control, and in your self-control, perseverance, and in your perseverance, godliness, and in your godliness, brotherly kindness, and in your

---

[101] Matthew 25:14-29
[102] John 15:1-8
[103] Matthew 21:18-21

brotherly kindness, love. For if these qualities are yours and are increasing, they render you neither useless nor unfruitful in the true knowledge of our Lord Jesus Christ."[104]

I know no man who sets out to be useless and unfruitful, and yet it is the end of so many because they lack diligence in the use of their gifts.

5. The Gifts need to be discovered and perfected.

Finally we should note that the gifts of God in our life need to be discovered and perfected by the believer. When you received your spiritual gifts you did not receive a list of instructions to accompany them. Rather you are given throughout your life opportunities to discover those gifts. Most of us discovered by accident the gifts in our lives. We stumbled on to them while singing in the shower, or talking with a friend. For this reason it is imperative that you take the opportunities you get to discover what may be hidden within your life for divine use. Andy Bilhorn writes in an article about discovering spiritual gifts that there are three practices you should consider in discovering your gifts. They are "self-reflection, practice, and community."[105]

Self-reflection is an honest look at yourself and your gifts and evaluating the results. Maybe you want to do something but are not very good at it, it may not be your gift. The sooner you recognize that, the sooner you will be able to move on to finding your true gifts. This is a prayerful process of determining what is the highest and best use of your abilities. I enjoy singing, and can carry a tune sometimes. But it's not my greatest gift to the body of Christ.

Practice is the next thing to consider. Try things. Try homeless ministry, serve at a nursing home, volunteer at children's church. Along the way you will find out what you are gifted at, and will be able to eliminate that you are not gifted at. The more you practice the more you will discover about yourself

---

[104] 2 Peter 1:5-8
[105] Bilhorn, Andy. "How to Discover Your Spiritual Gifts." RELEVANT Magazine. N.p., 23 May 2013. Web. 17 Jan. 2017.

and your gift.

Then there comes the all-important value of community. When you practice the gifts you have been given in the community of faith, it creates an environment for growth and encouragement. "All of the gifts are intended to be practiced in the context of community. You can't discover your spiritual gifts apart from community."[106]

Service

Paul then uses the second category of service. This word "service" is often translated as "ministry" or "administration." But the Greek word used here by Paul is actually the word "diakonia," from which we derive the word deacon. We might better understand its meaning by using our modern word "waiter." Literally a "diakonia" is one who waits on tables, or a domestic servant. In other words God has not just given us gifts, but he has also called us employ those gifts by waiting on tables through our service. The tables we wait on are as diverse as our gifts.

I personally serve as the waiter behind the pulpit of Kingsway Church. I strive weekly to serve the best spiritual food in the most relevant way possible to meet my flocks needs. For others their table is a hospital where they serve the sick with needed medicine and attention. Others serve at the table of education, or finance. Some literally serve tables in restaurants and cafes. As many are the needs of man and the purposes of God, as are the number of waiters God has anointed to serve.

Jesus taught us this principle by saying, "You know that the rulers of the Gentiles lord it over them, and their great men exercise authority over them. It is not this way among you, but whoever wishes to become great among you shall be your servant, and whoever wishes to be first among you shall be your slave; just as the Son of Man did not come to be served (diakoneo), but to serve (diakoneo), and to give His [n]life a ransom for many."[107]

---

[106] Bilhorn, Andy. "How to Discover Your Spiritual Gifts." RELEVANT Magazine. N.p., 23 May 2013. Web. 17 Jan. 2017.
[107] Matthew 20:25-28

We see here the great and fundamental difference between the kingdoms of this world and that of the Kingdom of God.

During the American Revolution a man in civilian clothes rode past a group of soldiers repairing a small defensive barrier. their leader was shouting instructions, but making no attempt to help them. Asked why by the rider, he retorted with great dignity, 'Sir, I am a corporal!' The stranger apologized, dismounted, and proceeded to help the exhausted soldiers. The job done, he turned to the corporal and said, 'Mr. Corporal, next time you have a job like this and not enough men to do it, go to your commander-in-chief, and I will come and help you again.' It was none other than George Washington.[108]

Franklin Roosevelt's closest adviser during much of his presidency was a man named Harry Hopkins. During World War II, when his influence with Roosevelt was at its peak, Hopkins held no official Cabinet position. Moreover, Hopkins's closeness to Roosevelt caused many to regard him as a shadowy, sinister figure. As a result he was a major political liability to the President.

A political foe once asked Roosevelt, "Why do you keep Hopkins so close to you? You surely realize that people distrust him and resent his influence." Roosevelt replied, "Someday you may well be sitting here where I am now as President of the United States. And when you are, you'll be looking at that door over there and knowing that practically everybody who walks through it wants something out of you. You'll learn what a lonely job this is, and you'll discover the need for somebody like Harry Hopkins, who asks for nothing except to serve you." Winston Churchill rated Hopkins as one of the half-dozen most powerful men in the world in the early 1940s. And the sole source of Hopkins's power was his willingness to serve."[109]

In the kingdoms of this world, the ruler lords over his subordinates with impunity. They exist for his comfort and ease. The thought of "waiting tables" or serving those less fortunate is

---

[108] Today in the Word, March 6, 1991
[109] Discipleship Journal, Issue 39 (1987), p. 5.

foreign to his thinking. Sitting perched in great material success and social influence he thinks himself something great. He says, I'm a Corporal, I'm a Reverend, I'm an Administrator, or a Statesman. And yet Jesus would call that ruler a failure because he failed to use his office to serve others. Then Jesus looks you and me in the eye and says "It is not this way among you."[110] As if to say "I expect more from my kids."

He expects more from us because he taught us by his own example. The Son of Man did not come to be waited on, but to be a waiter. And to exhaust that service through the ultimate sacrifice of his life in exchange for others. Jesus, as General George Washington who dismounted his horse to serve with his men, so Christ in an infinity greater way, stepped down from glory to wait on a table we call the cross. Here in is true biblical success. As a closing thought we might reflect on the words of the Presbyterian Pastor A.T. Pierson who wrote:

The supreme test of service is this: For whom am I doing this? Our work must again be tested by three propositions: Is it work from God, as given us to do from Him; for God,   as   finding   in Him its secret of power; and with God, as only a part of His work in which we engage as co-workers with Him.[111]   What is your table?

Effects

Then we see that this diversity extends a variety of effects. The Greek word used here for effect is the word "energema," from which we get our word, energy. Literally the word effect implies that God gives us the "energy and ability" to carry out His will. The spirit works in us by giving us the energy or vitality needed to affect His intended result. Another way of saying it, is that He gives us the ability to "do" the work which he has intended for us to do. Paul writes to the Philippian believers saying that "It is God who is at work in you, both to will and to do for His good pleasure."[112] This is a powerful truth deserving our full attention.

---

[110] Matthew 20:26
[111] A.T. Pierson wrote, The Truth.
[112] Philippians 2:13

Apart from the Spirit, man lacks the will to serve God. His mind is preoccupied by secular concerns. And apart from the anointing man though he may want to serve the Lord finds that he has neither the energy or ability to do so. Therefore in giving his indwelling Spirit to man, God enables him first of all the will to serve the Lord and then also the ability to do so. There is nothing God has called you to do, which God has not also given you the energy and ability by His Sprit to do it. This is the great promise of the anointing. The anointing is absolutely effective, and makes us effective in our service to Christ.

This is a recurring theme in the Apostle Paul's writings. His letters are full of the constant affirmation that something is operating in him, which is greater than he is, and which has marvelous effect. This something is nothing less than the anointing of the Holy Spirit. Paul further states in the same letter "I can do all things through Him who strengthens me."[113] And he writes to the Colossian believers "For this purpose also I labor, striving according to His power, which mightily works within me."[114] And yet again he prays for the Ephesians asking God to "Strengthen them with Power through His Spirit in the inner man."[115]

It is therefore imperative that we walk daily in this assurance, that God has granted through His indwelling Spirit the "energy and ability" to do what he called us to do. This comes from God, and is enabled by our faith.

Now we note that the gifts are numerous, because the places where we must serve are diverse. Under the anointing, each person will manifest this diversity. It seems that the anointing is one of the least understood factors in ministry success. Yet it is indispensable to it.

The anointing of God on a life, makes ministry easy, grants spiritual authority, and supernatural ability. The anointing is the hand of God upon the gifts of God in your life. Without the anointing, man wields God's gifts around like a heavy implement

---

[113] Philippians 4:13
[114] Colossians 1:29
[115] Ephesians 3:16

of battle in a clumsy and ineffective manner. But with the anointing, the gift becomes weightless and you become agile in the exercise of their use.

I am a preacher, so I am naturally inclined to discuss the anointing in preaching, but I readily admit that that is too narrow a focus. You see, the anointing isn't just for preachers in the pulpit, it's for businessmen and businesswomen in the board room as well. The anointing is for mothers in their child-rearing years, and for teachers in the classroom. The anointing of God is for every believer, anywhere, and any occupation, in order to accomplish divine objectives.

One of the most fascinating observations of this is in the life of Eric Liddell. A Missionary martyr to China, who also happened to be an Olympic Gold Medalist. He was once quoted as saying "I believe God made me for a purpose, but He also made me fast, and when I run, I feel His pleasure."[116] That is such a good description of the anointing. Eric recognized that God had called Him to win souls in China, and that he did with great effect. But he also recognized that God's hand was also upon his other gifts as well, and in yielding to that anointing He brought great pleasure to God.

What's Your "Because"

As we discuss the anointing we must keep in mind that the anointing is given in order to accomplish a divine objective. Jesus at the beginning of his preaching ministry in Nazareth laid out the purpose of his ministry, and explained the power for that purpose. He said "The spirit of the Lord God is upon me, because he has anointed me to preach good news to the poor."

Notice the use of the word "because." Jesus is saying that the anointing was on him "because" of the work he had been sent to do. The preaching of the Gospel, the recovery of sight to the blind, the healing of the broken hearted and the liberating of captives were all the "because" of His life. This necessitate the anointing. Until you discover your "because" or your purpose, you won't understand you need for the anointing.

---

[116] Eric Liddell

We have a glimpse of this in the life of David, on the occasion of his showdown with Goliath. When David came on the scene Goliath had been taunting the armies of Israel for 40 days. No one dared challenge the giant, until a little boy fresh of the farm showed up with an anointing on his life. Some days or maybe months before David had been anointed King of Israel by the prophet Samuel.

With his hair still oily from the anointing of Samuel, the boy David asked, "Who is this uncircumcised Philistine that he should defy the armies of the living God?"[117] When he was rebuked by his elder brother for meddling in men's business David famously answered "is there not a cause?"[118] I imagine that deep within David's soul he understood that the Anointing upon his life, was not without purpose. This was his cause and he would not shirk it in the day of opportunity. Do you know what your "because" is?

Note also the preposition "to." The anointing comes "to" or "towards" some purpose. Just as you don't put gas in a parked car, so God does not anoint men who are not going "towards" a divine assignment. If you remain on assignment, you can expect the anointing to carry it out.

"For whoever has, to him more shall be given, and he will have an abundance; but whoever does not have, even what he has shall be taken away from him."[119] The more you use the anointing in your life, the more you will have of it to use. The anointing on your life aims you like an arrow "towards" the purpose of God.

In 2 Kings 4:6 we read about a widow who was about to lose her sons into slavery on account of her late husband's unpaid debts. The prophet Elisha instructed her borrow more than a few empty jars, and pour into them the last jar of oil she had left in her house. As she poured the oil from her jar, into the jars of others the oil miraculously began to fill each jar. So long as she had jars to fill, she had oil to fill them. But when she ran out of jars, "the oil stopped"[120] flowing.

---

[117] 1 Samuel 17:26
[118] 1 Samuel 17:29

This is a principle we cannot afford to overlook. The anointing demands usefulness, and so long as we will find vessels into which to pour our gifts we will have the endless supply of anointing. The only thing that can explain a dead church, or a spiritually dead Christian is the lack of useful aim toward the purpose of God.

This is a tragic reality among many churches that have experienced revival and spiritual outpouring. Where the anointing was truncated and reserved merely as an experience it eventually stops flowing. Yet where the anointing is seen as means to God ends, you will find that it continues to flow without end.

---

[120] 2 Kings 4:8

Chapter 9

Things I've Learned About The Anointing

But you have an anointing from the Holy One,
and you all know. 1 John 2:20

In the early 90s Pastor Jack Hayford of the Church On The Way shared a vision with his congregation in a Sunday morning service. He said that while he was praying he saw a vision of Jesus seated upon a throne. In the vision Jesus began to stand, and as he stood, oil began to fall out from the folds of his robes. This was the oil that had been poured out upon the head of the Messiah the anointed one. Pastor Hayford further stated that this was the anointing that God was pouring out on the last days. This vision, like all visions and dreams, must be taken in light of Scripture. And I believe that is presents us with a vivid image of a vital truth. The oil which falls upon the church today, is that which belongs to the Christ.

Our Anointing, if it is anointing at all, must come from Jesus. The only reason that the Holy Spirit can come upon us is because we are in Christ. Just as his righteousness is our righteousness, having none of our own. So His anointing is our anointing, because we have none of our own. Everything that we receive from God must be received by faith. We were saved by faith, we are being sanctified by faith, we will be glorified by faith. We receive the baptism in the Holy Spirit by faith, and we operate in the anointing of the Spirit by faith as well. This faith must rest on the person of Jesus Christ.

In the twenty eight-years that I have been preaching, I have learned a few truths concerning the anointing which I believe have served me well and are supported by scripture.

Christ Is the Source of the Anointing

The First truth that I have learned about the Anointing, and perhaps the most important, is that Christ is the source of the anointing. This is precisely the most important truth you can learn on this subject. There is no anointing outside of Christ. He said, "I will ask the Father, and He will give you another Helper, that He may be with you forever; that is the Spirit of truth, whom the world cannot receive, because it does not see Him or know Him, but you know Him because He abides with you and will be in you."[121] John the Baptist said that when Jesus came Jesus would "baptize in the Holy Spirit."[122] And John writes in his epistle saying "As for you, the anointing which you received from Him abides in you."[123]

Perhaps this does not sound like a great revelation, but the fact is that often the simplest things can be ignored. This truth is essential for us, because the anointing does not come from any other source, nor does it emanated from any work which a man may do. Christ is the Anointed one. That is what the word "Christ" means. Therefor those who desire to live and serve in the power of the anointing must be connected to the "Anointed One." Apart from Christ there is no anointing, and apart from faith in Him, we cannot enjoy his power.

---

[121] John 14:16-17
[122] John 1:33
[123] 1 John 2:27

Only in Christ do we have any hope of the anointing. And by extension, in Christ we have great access to the anointing of the Holy Spirit. This cannot possibly be over stated. Jesus is the source of the anointing, therefore our connection to Him is vital. Often a mistake that beginning preachers make is that they copy what they perceive to be the anointing in someone else. I'm not saying we should not have role models, because that is very important. You cannot obtain by copying what God has given another person. The anointing as we have already stated is God's hand on our gift. Whether in vocational ministry or in the marketplace, you must be you, and rely on Christ to provide His anointing on your gifts and then abide in that anointing.

Jesus said "Abide in Me, and I in you. As the branch cannot bear fruit of itself unless it abides in the vine, so neither can you unless you abide in Me. "I am the vine, you are the branches; he who abides in Me and I in him, he bears much fruit, for apart from Me you can do nothing."[124] These simple instructions hold the key to useful and fruitful ministry. Apart from the anointing of Christ on our gifts, we can bear no fruit.

The Old Testament hero named Samson may shed great light on this truth. Samson was a Judge of Israel and has great exploits for God ascribed to his name. Four times the scriptures tell us of Samson's anointing. The first time is in Judges 13:25. We read that "the Spirit of the Lord began to stir him at times."[125] There we read a simple phrase which implies a great working of God on the life of a young Samson. The Spirit of the Lord "stirred" him from time to time. There he was, a young man growing into his call, and God would stir or agitate his inner man with a desire to act on behalf of God.

Perhaps you have felt the stirring of the Spirit, an inner urgency to do something, to correct some wrong, or to alleviate some burden. An inner impulse to do something about the things you see around you. This did not originate with Samson, or with you. This is a divine act whereby a man is acted upon by an outside force. Acted upon by the blazing fire of Gods desire to use

[124] John 15:4-5
[125] Judges 13:25

the instrument of His choosing. Some flee from it in terror; others yield to it in hope of bringing God His glory.

Then in Judges 14:6 we read that while Samson was traveling one day a "young lion came roaring towards him." Perhaps surprised by the unforeseen danger, Samson suddenly found himself overcome by a superior courage and strength. The text says that "the spirit of the Lord rushed upon him."

As quickly as a lion charging his prey, came this rush of anointing upon Samson. What had once stirred him, now empowered him to act in a miraculous way. Samson tore the lion to pieces with his bear hands because of the "rush."

Interestingly, the New Testament uses the same word "rush" to describe the coming of the Holy Spirit on the early church. Acts says that *"suddenly there came from heaven a noise like a violent, rushing wind."*[126] In both cases two facts emerge. First that God's man is acted upon by an outside force as we saw previously. Secondly, the word "rush" implies that this force produces profitable action.

Do you want your actions to be profitable? Do you want what you do for God to be fruitful? Then you need the anointing of the Holy Spirit upon your gifts. The anointing of the Holy Spirit will produce fruitful action. It will turn a leisurely stroll into a bold stand for God's glory. It will move you to action, and that action will be effective.

Twice more we read that the Lord moved in this way on Samson. And each time to great effect for the glory of God. Oh how we need the "rushing" of the Spirit upon the Church today. So many today stroll through their Christian life making no impact for God on their generation. Others dream of doing something for God someday! They need desperately a move of God upon their hearts. Let this be the prayer of every Christian today, "Rush upon us oh God, that we may act on your behalf."

I wish that I could end Samson's story here. But the truth is

---

[126] Acts 2:2

that this man though mightily anointed, failed ultimately to abide in the source of that anointing. For Samson the simple injunction which guaranteed him his strength was "the Nazarite vow." As a Nazarite there were three things he was not to do under any circumstances. First he was not drink any wine or strong drink. Second, he was not to eat any unclean thing. And third, he was not to cut his hair. That was the cost of abiding in the Anointing he was given.

As we read the book of Judges we find that he violated each of these simple commands. Through the process of systematic compromise the anointed man of God cast off each restraint one at a time. Finally his hair was cut, and we read the tragic verdict "He did not know that the Lord had departed from Him."[127]

I doubt you've ever thought of Samson's hair in relation to Christ. But it's an interesting analogy which we should not ignore. His anointing was not in his hair, it was in what his hair represented. For Samson, the keeping of his hair was an outward symbol of the fact that he remained connected to the source of his anointing. To cut his hair was to sever the ties which he had to the God who "stirred" him in the first place.

Today our connection to Christ does not consist of any external symbol or even our ability to keep a vow. Because of the grace of God we are not saved by any work or merit of our own. Our connection to God exists purely through faith in Christ. As we rest in that vital life-giving relationship, we can expect the anointing to flow though our lives.

Samson's story took a devastating turn. He lost his anointing and found himself in bondage to his enemy. Don't ever underestimate the high cost of sin. His eyes were gouged out, leaving him blind. He was put to slavery in a grinding mill, losing his freedom. He was put to shame before the Philistines, losing his dignity. Such is the result of disconnection from the anointing. Perhaps you find yourself in that place, without vision, without freedom, and without honor.

---

[127] Judges 16:20

Maybe like Samson you have been disconnected from the source of spiritual power in your life. Samson's story did not end there and neither does yours. Because the scripture states that "the hair of his head began to grow again."[128] This was the Holy Spirits subtle way of informing us that while things were down for Samson there was a slow but steady regrowth of faith. So long as you return to the source of the anointing, and allow healing to take place in your heart, I am convinced that you too can experience the faith that will restore and empower you once again.

God Will Not Anoint The Flesh

The second truth about the anointing is that God will not anoint the flesh. No matter how well intentioned our efforts may be, if they are works of the flesh they will fail for lack of anointing. It is an invariable aspect of God's nature that he will not share his glory with the flesh. I know we are used to hearing the word flesh in connection with sinful practices like immortality, insobriety, outbursts of anger, violence, etc. But the fact is that a work of the flesh is anything that we do apart from faith.

In Romans 8, we read that "The flesh cannot please God." And in Hebrews 11 we read that "Without faith it is impossible to please God." Thus faith nor flesh is the key to the flow of the anointing in our lives.

If I preach a sermon where I depend on my knowledge, craft, oratory, and charisma, I am speaking from the strength of my flesh. I may move emotions and stir thought, but the fruit will be that of a self-delivered speech. This, God will not anoint. This is true in any area of ministry. The preacher, worship leader, or Sunday school teacher. Anyone who leans on what s/he knows is drawing from the exhaustible well of self-effort and is limited. But when God's man brings his gift and makes it a servant of the Lord, laying down his reliance on himself, and simply says "Lord I need your anointing on my gifts today. I don't have what it takes to break the yoke that's on the people. My oratory and education are inadequate to the task." When he yields his gifts to God, he sets his flesh aside and becomes a candidate for the Anointing of the

---

[128] Judges 16:22

Holy Spirit. Now his gifts are an asset because they are yielded to the anointing of the Holy Spirit.

For many years now I have followed a pattern in my preaching ministry. I prepare to preach diligently in prayer. Trying earnestly to hear from the Lord what he would say, and once I have heard from him I prepare my sermon. I read everything I can that I think might help me express what I heard from God. I try to look at the text from every vantage point, and pray through how I can present it in a way that the child and the scholar may understand.

I do my homework as it were. I dig and dig in researching, reading, writing, and practicing. Then when it time to preach, I try to always go before the Lord and say "Lord, I have nothing to set before your people today, if you don't speak through me I don't have a word. I yield myself to you, and I receive your anointing by faith." Some days I miss the mark, but many times I feel as though in some way God has gotten through to his people, and His anointing has made all the difference.

My father had a way with my brothers and me. We were often ministering together in a service. And if he sensed that there was no anointing on the service, or that we were holding back the flow of the anointing in any way, he would turn around and tell us in a stern tone "Get in the Spirit!" It wasn't exactly a dissertation on eighth chapter of Romans, but it got the point across. He was saying "get into faith." Those four words taught us that we had to switch over from self-reliance to faith. Only then would the anointing flow unhindered.

As Paul taught the Corinthians, spiritual things must "spiritually appraised." They cannot be entered into, enjoyed, or shared by the flesh. Since you are in Christ, you have an anointing. That anointing is equal to the task, but it will lie dormant until you engage it by faith.

God's word is the only message God will anoint

Finally, I believe I can say without fear of contradiction, that God's word is the only message God will anoint. This point I've learned specifically as a preacher, and hope to share with my counterparts in the preaching ministry. The pulpit is an interesting place. And the 21st Century pulpit has come under gross attack in recent years. There is a great and mounting pressure on the preacher to preach a message that satisfies the itching ears of man.

The church today is frequented by "church shoppers" who treat the house of God like a local restaurant. On any given Sunday morning you will find them deciding between attending church or doing more important duties. And if they decide to attend services, they then decide which flavor of service they are interested in. Perhaps a quiet liturgical mood will draw them one Sunday. But at other times they want a motivational message to face a tough week. Like choosing a restaurant, they choose a church.

This can and has placed a great deal of pressure of pastors. Perhaps it is because they need to play to a particular mood or crowd in order to please men. Some have abandoned the Bible all together, preaching from the thoughts of self-help teachers and sages of the new age. This has led many to fall short of their call to "Preach the Word" in season and out of season. I can't blame them; after all I have felt the same pressures from time to time. But one truth has remained in my heart, and kept me from deviating. That is that in my experience the only message which the Holy Spirit will anoint is the Bible and the Gospel of Jesus Christ.

No matter how eloquent or articulate a thought may be, if it does not draw its truth from Scripture it will enjoy none of Scriptures power. The word of God is anointed in and of its self. It bears the attribute of animation, meaning that it is endued with life. The writer of Hebrews tells us that the "word of God is living and active."[129]

For all of the art of Shakespeare and the philosophy of Locke their writings boast of no such power. God's word alone is living and active. Paul wrote of the Words effect saying "You received from us the word of Gods message, you accepted it not as the word

---

[129] Hebrews 4:12

of men, but for what it really is, the word of God, which also performs its work in you who believe."[130]

God's Word performs its work in those who believe. There is no single parcel of writing anywhere in the world, ancient or modern, that has such power to perform. For this reason God will not anoint the preaching of any savior but Christ, any message but the Gospel, any book but the Bible. Read all the Christian books you like, hear all the sermons you like, only be sure that their truth emanates from the truth found in God's inspired Word.

---

[130] 1 Thessalonians 2:13

Chapter 10

Joseph:
A Type of
Christ

He sent a man before them, even Joseph, who was sold for a servant: Whose feet they hurt with fetters: he was laid in iron: Until the time that his word came: the word of the LORD tried him. The king sent and loosed him; even the ruler of the people, and let him go free. He made him lord of his house, and ruler of all his substance. Psalm 105:17-21

      The Old Testament is filled with types and shadows of the Lord Jesus Christ. Types are teachings and often prophecies hidden in plain sight. The men and women of the old testament lived out their lives without realizing that they were often foreshadowing the Messiah. This underling thread of revelation is woven throughout all the Scriptures and has been called the Scarlet Thread of Redemption. We find this scarlet thread in the lives of men like Aaron, Able, Adam, David, Isaac, Joseph, Joshua, Melchizedek, and Moses to name a few. However the life of Joseph is perhaps the most complete type of Christ in the Old Testament. The contrast between the two men is incredible to behold, and when you understand the fact the Joseph went into Egypt as a forerunner to save his family from the coming famine, you will also understand that Christ did the same for all mankind in going to the cross. In fact the parallels between to the life of Joseph and the life Jesus are an excellent example of the inspiration of the Bible, and the miraculous nature of their lives.

There are no sins recorded against Joseph in the scriptures, which point to the fact that he was a shadow of the sinless Christ who was to come. Joseph we do know did sin, he was a man like any other, but there was no sin recorded against him. He figures for us the sinless perfection of Christ who the scriptures state that "he knew no sin."[131] Even Pontius Pilate when he tried Jesus said "I find not fault in him"[132] His life was lived without sin, because only a sinless sacrifice could atone for man.

Both Joseph and Jesus were born through a miracle of special intervention. In the case of Joseph God intervened giving the barren Rachel ability to conceive. In the case of Christ the miracle was much greater as it required a virgin conception in the womb of Mary.

Both were the special object of their fathers love, and the objects of hate by their brothers. Both were stripped of their robes, and placed in a pit unto death. Both take Gentile brides, and in graft a gentile people into their family. Joseph married an Egyptian and Christ will marry his Church. Both were humiliated before being exalted. Paul states in 1 Corinthians 10:11 that "these things were given for our examples." Thus we can gain from Joseph a valuable insight into the glory and worth of our Lord.

I will Go

At the beginning of this story we find, Jacob sending Joseph to check on the welfare of His brothers who had gone to tend their flocks. Because of their history, Joseph must have known that his brothers would be in a wrong place. If they were in the wrong place he was duty bound to report it to his father. And if he

---

[131] 2 Corinthians 5:21
[132] John 18:38

reported them, they were going to hate him even more than they hated him already. He had to have known that his brothers were going to see him coming, and that there hate would make him a target, perhaps he even knew that they might not come back to Jacob, yet he answered "I will Go."

One can only wonder what that must have been like, when before the foundation of the world the Holy Trinity had the ultimate conversation. Sin was the problem, and souls were in the balance. It was in this moment that the Son of God, would say "I will Go." He knew that his brothers would see him coming, and deny His purpose, while plotting His end. He must have known that he would be bruised and put to grief, and that His soul would be offered as an offering for sin.

He knew that he would be blasphemed, and slandered. He knew that would be wounded for our transgressions and bruised for iniquity. He must have known that he would be rejected by those he came to save. He must have seen the desolation of his body on the Cross. He must have known that in a moment of divine disgust, the relationship between God the Son, and God the Father, would be severed, and he must have known that he would cry out, "My God why, have you forsaken me." And yet He said "I WILL GO."

When Joseph's brothers saw him coming they conspired to kill him, saying, "We'll see what will become of his dream." The stripped him of his tunic, and threw him in a pit. With regard to Christ, this was not only fulfilled in the process of crucifixion, but is still being attempted to this day. Hebrews 10:29 stated that "they trampled underfoot the Son of God, counting the blood of the covenant a common thing."

The world since the day of Christ, has tried to strip the Son of God, trampling underfoot his blood. Men still today, attempt to strip Jesus of His divinity, suggesting that he was only a mere man. Others try to strip Him of His Soverety, claiming that he is a mere mortal. Still others try to strip Him of His relevance, keeping His name from pulpits and lecterns alike. The Da Vinci Code tried to strip him of His holiness, by claiming that he faked his own death, and concealed a sexual relationship. Liberal theologians have tried to strip him of the "power of His resurrection" by claiming that he is still in the grave.

Yet one more level of understanding can be reached, that being that Christ in His Sovereignty, stripped himself of his own robe. Paul writes in Philippians 2:6, "who, although he existed in the form of God, did not regard equality with God a thing to be grasped, but emptied Himself, taking the form of a bond servant, and being made in the likeness of men." Of what did he empty himself, surly neither of his omnipresence, omnipotence, nor his omniscience Rather it was the empting of himself of his "pre-incarnate" glory. As in the words of J.B. Lightfoot, "Laying aside the insignia for majesty," becoming a carpenter's son. (Ps 45:8)

> My Lord has garments so wondrous fine,
> and myrrh their texture fills;
> its fragrance reached to this heart of mine,
> with joy my being thrills.

> Out of the Ivory palaces
> Into a world of woe,
> Only His great eternal love
> Made my savior go.

Joseph's brothers stripped him of what they feared. They stripped him, to sooth their own conscience and attempt to avoid what seemed evident to all. Indirectly this is the same reason for which men attempt to strip Christ of his position. For inherently they're conscience testifies against them that His is God, that He is Holy, and the He will Judge all men. For this reason Paul writes that "men suppress the truth...because that which is known about God is evident within them."

All of these attempts are man's desperate endeavor to deny what he knows deep down is true, "there is a God and I am accountable to Him." Thus if one denies his sin, he can also deny the One who called it sin in the first place. This is the aim of secular humanism and the new age, everything is relative, nothing is concrete, and there are no absolutes. What could drive men to such horror, to sell their brother as a slave? Seeking only to rid their soul of the hate they harbored against him. It is here where we see the brothers unfurl their elaborate deception. They took the coat and dipped it in goat's blood, and brought it to Jacob, saying "do you know if this is your son's coat." Allowing Jacob to draw the conclusion "Joseph is dead."

God is Dead

19th century German philosopher Friedrich Nietzsche may have done more to perpetrate a similar hoax on our time than any other. "God is dead," Nietzsche said, "and we have killed him. How shall we, murderers of all murderers, console ourselves?"

The great tragedy of our time is that we are living the practical results of Nietzsche's philosophical speculations. By suggesting that "God is dead" he removed the moral influence from over man's mind. This is the "grand" end of atheism; man can live as he wills, and worry not about his end. Modern man spews out diatribe against any suggestion of God, claiming that there is no absolute truth. Rather, that there is no one truth that is true for all. In a somewhat humorous article Steve Turner writes the following in Nice and Nasty describing the creed of modern man...

"We believe in Marx, Freud, and Darwin. We believe everything is OK as long as you don't hurt anyone, to the best of your definition of hurt, and to the best of your knowledge We believe in sex before during and after marriage. We believe in the therapy of sin. We believe that adultery is fun. We believe that sodomy's OK. We believe that taboos are taboo. We believe that everything's getting better despite evidence to the contrary. The evidence must be investigated. You can prove anything with evidence."

Turner then adds this jarring statement "If chance be the Father of all flesh, disaster is his rainbow in the sky, and when you hear: State of Emergency! Sniper Kills Ten! Troops on Rampage! Youths go Looting! Bomb Blasts School! It is but the sound of man worshiping his maker."

When we look at the results of such a worldview, where God is dead, and moral absolutes are neither moral nor absolute, we cannot help but be disturbed. It was Nietzsche's work which Adolph Hitler used to perpetrate his "Super Man" doctrine, resulting in the death of millions. It was this worldview which moved Lennon and Stalin to suppress generations of men in the grip of Soviet Atheism. Bloodshed upon bloodshed is the argument of this worldview, and the trend of our generation. Auschwitz, Belzec, and Majdanek are the greatest evidence against such worldview. History cries out against this madness, and modern man is too drunk with self-exalting passions that he cannot hear her cries.

What is Truth

After Jesus was betrayed by Judas, he was taken to be tried, by the Sanhedrin, Harod, and Pontius Pilate. While being tried in the presence of Pontius Pilate, Jesus was asked this provoking question, "What is truth?" Then Pilate left the room. This seems to be the attitude of modern man toward this question, asking, but not waiting for the answer. What is truth? In John 14:6 Jesus said "I am the way, the truth, and the life." In this one statement Jesus denied to claims of every other world religion. His statement was exclusive, particular, and singular. For a world pretending to seek truth, the answer is not a "what," rather a "who." And that who said "I am the truth."

Just as we know from hindsight that Joseph's "death" would open the door for the salvation of the very ones who had sold him into slavery. We know that the death of Christ would open the door of salvation for the very human race which had rejected him.

Joseph is Yet Alive

A great many year years have passed since Joseph was sold, space has not allowed us to delve into the great depth of wisdom which can be found in the trials faced by Joseph, from the pit to the palace. However we arrive at the moment when the whole of his challenge finally makes since. For Joseph this must have been a moment of indescribable joy and sorrow. When to his feet, fell those men who were his brother, whose deeds had made him a slave, a prisoner, and prince. Joy in the knowledge that God had used their wickedness to save them, sorrow in the knowledge of their desperate plight. All of his life was poised for this moment. Every moment of brokenness, and shame, every bit of anger, and frustration with his God, culminated on this day.

Just as Joseph had foretold, a famine had come upon the land and Jacob and his sons were to be casualties in its wake. The glory of this story is too great to be told, as one looks at mankind dying of spiritual hunger, longing to sooth their empty soul. In this horror of reality, where the vultures of sin lurk about waiting to feast on the carcass of man's lost eternal soul.

In this state of being, where those who are dying don't have enough since know that they are dying, Christ comes to become the bread of Life. As the tribe of some seventy people waited to die, Jacob receives news that there is grain in Egypt. He tells his sons to stop looking around waiting to die, and sends them to buy grain from this foreign governor. To be sure this was not an easy task, seeking to buy grain in a time of famine, from a government such as Egypt. But it is here where we see the gracious provision of the father, who sends Joseph ahead of his brothers to save their lives.

Paul states in Romans 5:8 that while we were yet sinners, Christ died for us in a demonstration of the Fathers love. While we were still idol worshipers, without regard to God and his law, murderers and thieves, liars and adulterers, Christ died for us. Before we knew the tragedy of sin, He became the "Lamb of God, slain from the foundation of the world."

What Difference does it make?

The Resurrection of Christ is the single most important fact in Bible History. If the Resurrection is not true, then the whole of our faith is useless. If Christ did not rise from the dead, then we ought to throw away our Bibles, shut down our churches, and burn our hymnal. Paul stated in 1 Cor 15:17 "If Christ be not raise, we are yet in our sins." Without the Resurrection of Christ, the Christian faith is a hoax, and ought to be demonstrated as such.

However, if the Resurrection of Christ is in fact true, as we believe, then it has vast and far reaching implications for the whole of humanity. The evidence for this historical fact is too vast to be covered appropriately in this article, but a few sources may be useful.

According to 1 Corinthians 15:17, there were more than five

hundred eye witnesses to the Resurrection, to this day eye witness testimony is considered one of the highest forms of evidence in a court of law. If over five hundred men and women had conspired to lie about these facts, then it seems reasonable to assume that considering the threat of life levied against them by Rome, the some would have renounced their claims for the sake of their own lives.

However, there is not historical evidence in sacred or secular writings, which so much as implies that any one of the "eye witnesses" renounced their story. Now for a brief proof from none interested parties. In the time of Christ there lived a historian by the name of Josephus who wrote the following concerning Jesus Christ.

Now there was about this time Jesus, a wise man if it be lawful to call him a man, for he was a doer of wonders, a teacher of such men as receive the truth with pleasure. He drew many after him both of the Jews and the gentiles. He was the Christ. When Pilate, at the suggestion of the principal men among us, had condemned him to the cross, those that loved him at the first did not forsake him, for he appeared to them alive again the third day, as the divine prophets had foretold these and then thousand other wonderful things about him, and the tribe of Christians, so named from him, are not extinct at this day (Antiquities 18:63-64).

If Christ is indeed raised from the dead, then the first implication is that He is who He claimed to be. In Luke 22:70 he claimed to be the Son of God, in John 6:35 he claimed to the bread of life, and in John 8:58 he claimed to have existed before Abraham. In John 9:5 he claimed to be the Light of the world, the Door of the Sheep in John 10:7, the Good Shepherd in John 10:11, the Resurrection and Life in John 11:25, and the Way, the Truth, the Life, in John 14:6. All of these claims point to the deity of Christ, a fact sealed by the truth of His resurrection.

Additionally, the Resurrection demonstrates that God the Father accepted the sacrifice for sin offered on the Cross. Romans 4:25 stated the Christ was "raised again because of our Justification." Those who come in repentance to Christ have the overwhelming confidence that because Christ paid the price for sin and God the Father accepted it, no one now or ever shall be able to indict us of such crimes and he has already died to destroy.

Further the Resurrection assures believers their own resurrection. According to 1 Corinthians 15:20, "Christ has been raised from the dead, the first fruits of those who are asleep." Thus because he lives, we too shall live.

Finally, the Resurrection of Christ from the dead insures the world of coming judgment. In Acts 17 Paul speaking to the Philosophers at mars hill, declares that, God has established a day in which he will judge the world. He has established a man, who will be judge, and he verified his worthiness to judge, by raising that man; Christ Jesus from the dead.

One cannot over emphasize this point. There is a judgment day coming, in which all peoples, tribes, and tongue, men small and great, shall stand before the risen Son of God. His judgments will be accurate because He is a man, righteous because he is the Holy God, final because He is sovereign. The Resurrection is the stamp of finality on the summons of human existence. One may not enjoy a dinner with Queen Elizabeth; neither sit and talk with President Bush. But all will stand before the throne of God; all have a date with death, and after death judgment.

For the Christian there will be a judgment by fire, according to 2 Corinthians 5:10 in which our works will be tested. While this is not a judgment of heaven or hell, it will test our motives, our service, and our lives. It will be a test of the true worth of ones acts on earth, did one live for self or for God. The other judgment is altogether different, this is the Great White Throne, at which all who rejected Christ will stand, to be sentenced to eternal hell. With such assurances of coming judgment we are commanded to repent, and believe in the Son of God.

Chapter 11

A Call To Action

In place of your fathers will be your sons; You shall make them princes in all the earth. Psalm 45:16

A great deal is being said today about the Millennial Generation. Like people generations have personalities. The iPhone Generation as I like to call it can be defined as that generation born between 1982 and the early 2000's. They are at times known as "'Millennial's," "the Millennium Generations," "Generation Next," or "Generation Y." This generation is the most technological in history, and stands to inherit the dysfunction of "Generation X." This includes the breakdown of the traditional family, the redefinition of cultural norms, and an assault on Truth.

The views of a generations are most noticeable as the older members begin to enter into their twenties. Certain things can already be seen in this generation.

1. They are the most culturally diverse in History.
2. They are political progressives in their majority.
3. They do not consider texting, tweeting, or Facebook to be innovations.
4. They are the least religious of any generation previously studied.

Additionally the iPhone Generation is also the largest generation since WWII, meaning they are actually larger that the Baby Boomer Generation.

Issues Facing The iPhone Generation

Internet: When considering the iPhone Generation, it is impossible to overlook the influence of the internet. The World Wide Web has increased knowledge, removed walls of distance, and created an alternate since of community and reality.

This is a great and growing challenge to the youth worker, because the I Pod Generations view of community and reality has been defined by social media, leading to a scenario where a teen can have a conversation in sound bites with a perfect stranger, but can't have a meaningful conversation at the dinner table.

Barna Research Group – 39% of Parents and 27% of Teens expressed the frustration that technology has made it hard to have a conversation.

Thus the means of communications which were to have united us, have created deeper divisions than ever anticipated. This poses a challenge to the family, and the church which needs to be intentionally addressed.

The Role of The Church: The Church can do much by teaching on the management of technology within the family and the encouragement of activities which do not include technology.

Music: Music has always been an integral part of any culture. However the end of the 20th Century and the beginning of the 21st, introduced a new dynamic to the world of music. Up until the 1980's it was not uncommon for the adult and the teenage in the home to listen to and enjoy the same music. This began to change in the 80s and 90s, with the walk-men, then the personal CD Player. However the advent of the MP3 Player and the iPhone, have completely changed the face of music. It is now quite common to see Music used as a means of personal expressions, and often isolation.

Thus what once united a family around a single radio, or once rallied a generation around a single cause has now become an expression of individualism. This further defines the lines of separation between members of the family and the church.

Attitude: The iPhone Generation has been characterized by some as having an attitude of interference towards everything. They often have a "whatever" attitude. This is significant because when this attitude is applied to matters of "Truth" and morality, there is no cultural line of demarcation between good and evil.

It is not uncommon for teens to have a prolonged conversation on which burger joint is best, or which athlete is better. But on matters of Faith they demonstrate indifference. This seems to support an earlier contention that Reality has been redefined, and values have been turned on their heads.

Having said this, my personal experience in teaching the Scriptures to teens, has shed new light on another aspect of this issue. The iPhone Generations views of the Scripture, God, and Faith, are increasingly deepening. Thus it seems that when confronted with deep topics, and hard answers, this generation is ready to shake off the cloak of indifference in their pursuit of truth.

Family: The iPhone Generation is paying the greatest price for the breakdown of the family. Those of us who grew up in a "traditional family[133]" may be among the last of a disappearing breed. Most of the iPhone generation is more familiar with a "non-traditional" family. This means that a teen may be growing up in a single parent home, or may be being raised by a grandparent, or a foster parent. In other cases the home is made up of homosexual partners.

This undoubtedly presents an incredible challenge and opportunity to the church. A church filled with "traditional families" who welcome and make room for the "non-traditional family" may do more to serve the iPhone Generation, just by showing up, than every social agency in America.

---

[133] Traditional Family – a family with the original married parents, and their biological or adopted children.

Statistics on the Subject: "Marriage and Divorce" By BRG

78% of American Adults have been Married (this demonstrates that the idea of Marriage is still a social norm.)

33% of American Adults who have been married have been divorced at least once.

(This means that 25% of Adults 18 or older have gone through a divorce. This is true with in the church as well.) While Marriage is a social norm, the stigma associated with divorce has diminished.

Church: These days it seems that the church is the object of much blame for the ills of youth ministry, so it is necessary to focus for a moment on the problem.

Just on the numbers, we see that the Church is losing ground. While the population of the USA has increased by 18% since 1990 the church has steadily lost 3% in the same period of time. Thus not only is the American church not reaching new people, it is also losing those who grew up in church to begin with.

Studies show that the ages of 16-22, are critical for the Church because this is the age at which a person who grew up in church is most likely to "drop out."

It is well known that people leave church. This has always been true. But our purpose is to ask why? A Barna Study states six reasons for "why people leave church."

Six Reasons Why Young Adults Leave The Church

1. The Church seems over protective. (The Church adopts a policy that if its new, it must be bad.)

2. The Church seems Shallow. (The Church does not direct its self to hard issues, nor enable a genuine experience with God.)

3. The Church seems antagonistic to Science. (The Church seems to be behind the science of the day.)

4. The Church held simplistic views on sexuality. (The
    Church has ignored or simplified sexual issues, to the point
    of seeming out of date.)

5. The Exclusivity of Christianity. (The Church seems afraid of
    other beliefs.)

6. The church seemed unwelcoming to doubters. (Doubt is
    not allowed to be expressed or discussed.) *Barna Research
    Group*

The Church must respond to these issues, but must be careful
in doing so. In the first place we cannot abandon the issue in
hopes of its going away. But neither can we blur the lines of faith
and morality until they are indistinguishable. Our response must
be clear, bold, and un-intimidated.

A Response to #1. We must choose our battles wisely. The battle
over a hymnal verses a power point projector, I would suggest is less
significant than the Inspiration of Scripture. Taking risk is a part of the
churches history since the beginning, and where the lines of morality and
faith are not interfered with the church must be willing to be a little less
protective.

A Response to #2 If the church is seen as shallow, this is an
invitation to go deep, and we should not fail to RSVP. Surly it is easier to
pick up a "teachers manual" the night before bible study, and let
someone else tell you what to say and how to say it. But it might be more
beneficial to your hearer to take on the hard issues, and open a dialogue
about the existence of God, the boundaries of sexuality, or the hard
saying of Christ. If its depth they want, then we must jump into deep
waters and learn how to swim.

A Response to #3 - The idea that the church is Antagonistic to
Science has its answer in a bold faith which both claims and verifies that
it's is science that is antagonistic to the scriptures and it is the Scripture
which is ahead of the science.

A Response to #4 - On the issues of Sexuality the church must
approach the issues with gentleness and clarity. Making clear that sexual
immorality (fornication, adultery, homosexuality) is sin, but that God is
gracious to the sinner who repents. Under no circumstances should the
church adopt the view that one can continue in these practices, but while
laying the foundation of Holiness, extend the hand of grace.

149

A **Response to #5** - While the earth remains, the Christian Faith will remain an exclusive faith. Never can the church adopt an inclusive platform and maintain its claim to being Christian. The claim of Christ on our faith is exclusive of all others. This does not mean however that the church should be afraid to talk about these very real issues, and should be ready to give an answer.

A **Response to #6** - In line with the previous problem, the church must be welcoming to the doubter in so much as his desire is to find the truth. While being careful with those whose desire to sow the seed of unbelief.

Another study profiled in the book "Essential Church," by Thom Rainer, states a different set of reasons.

Top Ten Reasons Why 18-22 Year Old's

Drop Out of Church

1. Needed a break from church.
2. Church members where hypocritical.
3. Moved to College or Work.
4. Work gets in the way of Church.
5. Distance from Church was to great.
6. Busyness.
7. Loss of Connection to the Church.
8. Disagreement with Churches Doctrine.
9. Spending more time with friends.
10. Only going to please others.

In this study we see a slightly different set of reasons, but both point out what is missing in the iPhone Generations experience of church. The bottom line: The Church is no longer considered essential to the iPhone Generation. Whereas Church was an essential part of the previous generations life, the iPhone Generation is struggling with that commitment.

Thom Rainer profiles the 7 Sins of a Dying Church. In it he points out the seven attitudes most responsible for this loss of relevance to the iPhone Generation.

Seven Sins of a Dying Church

1. Doctrinal Delusion

2. Loss of Evangelistic Passion

3. Failure to be Relevant

4. Few Outward Focused Ministries

5. Conflict over Preferences

6. Prioritizing Comfort

7. Biblical Illiteracy

It is important to note that the very things which the modern critics of the church say are the problem, actually are the solution. For instance it has been alleged that if the church is to doctrinally devout, to passionate about conversions, or too reliant on the scriptures it will chase people away. Yet the statistics show that just the opposite is true.

The following statistics by Barna can offer some hope for us.

The *"American Faith Engagement As Children"* poll by Barna, gives us some encouraging news. The poll demonstrates that the regular participation of Teenagers in Church has a strong impact on their relationship to the church later in life. To add to this Rainer states in his book that of those "church dropouts" who come back to the church, those who were given a solid biblical foundation in their formative years were most likely to return.

Thus our answer to the problem is not a departure from Scriptures but rather a passionate commitment to them.

Other Statistics which may shed some light on this issue were reported by Dr. Lee Vulkich and the "Cool Church Survey." In this survey Christian Teens were asked to rank which factors that most influenced their commitment to the church.

Ten Factors That Influence Commitment to the Church

1. A Welcoming Atmosphere

2. Quality Relationships

3. A Senior Pastor who understands and loves teens

4. Preaching which answered Key Questions

5. Spiritual Growth

6. Fun Activities

7. Engaging Music and Worship

8. Quality Relationships with Adults

9. Multiple Opportunities to Lead and Serve

10. High-Tech Entertaining Ministry Approach

When we boil all of this down the iPhone Generation seems to be after a genuine experience with Christ and His Church. Furthermore they demonstrate that active, intentional, and genuine relationships with mentors and spiritual father is not only healthy but greatly by the Millennial Generation.

I was born in the confluence of two generations. I was born at the tail end of Generation X and in the birthing place of the Millennial Generations. There have been more changes in church life from my observation in the last ten years of my life, than in the first twenty-five combined. And I expect that there will be more change in the next five than in the previous ten.

I have witnessed the churches' transition from singing out of a hymnal to singing off of a screen. I have noted a remarkable change in preaching styles and content, and wonder where all of it will end. In the throws of this great shift I see great possibility for cooperation between two generations. Many modern Josephs are rising whose voices will be known and whose dreams must be cultivated. And many modern Jacobs will discover that their greatest impact will be in releasing the dreamers to their God appointed task. Who knows whether America's future like Egypt's hang on the shoulders of a well cultivated "son" who wears the coat his father gives him.

A Word to the modern Josephs

To the Millennial generation I write with the sincerest hope of your listening ear. Wear the coat your father gave you. Never be ashamed to wear God's favor as a mantle over your life. Stay near the cross of Christ, whose blood alone can grant you access to God and victory over sin. Abide daily in the anointing, because it will make you powerful in the face of every threat. Find a mentor and learn all you can. Remember that a college degree does not guarantee an education, only a teachable heart can do that. And honor your Spiritual Fathers in the Lord, because you may have many teachers but you will not have many fathers.

A Word to the Modern Jacobs

To you I write with the confidence that you will appreciate the urgency of your task. The millennial generation lacks fathers as no generation in history ever has. When the Roman Empire left its vast multitude of orphans in the ally's to die of exposer, the church took them in. Now one thousand years later we have an orphan problem in the broken spirit of many millennial crying to be taken in. The mandate of mentorship and fatherhood falls to all men in the church. But beyond responsibility it is an extraordinary privilege. For to us as fallen the joyous task of being kingmakers in the 21st Century. "In place of your fathers will be your sons; You shall make them princes in all the earth."[134] Let it not be said of us, that when the cry of fatherless sons was heard in the wind, the church had no fathers to answer the call.

---

[134] Psalm 45:16

Study Guide

Chapter 1   The Birth of a Dreamer

1. Where does the desire to increase come from? Is it from God?

2. What does Matthew 13:33 reveal about the Kingdom of God and increase?

3. "Absolutely everything that God establishes increases, and that is a powerful truth which we must appropriate by faith. We must walk daily in the revelation that increase belongs to us as we do Kingdom business." How are you appropriating this truth to your life and ministry today?

4. Why was Rachel's prayer misguided, and are you possibly falling into the same traps?

5. What does Proverbs 11:25 teach us about adding value to people?

6. Joseph added value to people everywhere he went, why is this significant? How are you adding value to the people around you?

Chapter 2 The Coat

1. When did Joseph begin to have prophetic dreams, and why is it significant?

2. What is the power of a fathers voice in a sons life?

3. What do we learn from Joshua's relationship with Moses?

4. Have you ever been in a holding pattern like Elisha, what lessons did you learn in that season? How did they prepare you for the future?

5. What was the significance of pouring water on Elijah's hands?

6. What is so important about circumcising sons?

Chapter 3 Does The Church Have No Sons

1. What does it mean to be a son?

2. What are the three results of our adoption into the family of God? How do these truths impact your life today?

3. How is Jesus the perfect model of Sonship? What can we learn from his example?

4. What can you learn from Jesus about being lost in the fathers love?

5. Are you committed to the fathers will? How do you live out that commitment on a daily basis?

6. Are you being shaped by the father's presence? How can you increase that in your life?

Chapter 4 The Coat of Divine Favor

1. How did Jacob demonstrate his favor toward Joseph, and what does that teach us about Gods favor toward us?

2. Define favor?

3. How does the word grace relate to the favor of God?

4. Why is a revelation of Gods favor so important?

5. 2 Corinthians 3:21-22 states "Corinthians saying "let no one boast in men. For all things belong to you, whether

Paul or Apollos or Cephas or the world or life or death or
things present or things to come; all things belong to you,
and you belong to Christ; and Christ belongs to God."
What does the phrase "all things belong to you" reveal
about our status as children of God?

6. In the parable of the Prodigal Son, why didn't the elder
   brother ever enjoy his father's estate? Are you enjoying
   all the benefits of being a child of God?

Chapter 5 Favor in the Life of Ruth

1. What does Ruth's story teach us about staying positioned for divine favor?

2. Every season has an end. How does this fact impact your life today, and your preparation for tomorrow?

3. What were Boaz's reasons for extending favor to Ruth? What does this teach us about obtaining the favor of God?

4. How does humility attract Gods favor?

5. Why is compassion linked to receiving the favor of God?

Chapter 6 Fit For the Palace

1. The favor of God brings promotion, but what is our role in retaining the position we have been promoted to? Have you ever been promoted beyond your preparation, how did you handle that situation?

2. What is the palace you have been called to work within?

3. Why is honoring the protocol of the palace so important?

4. What do we learn about excellence from the book of Daniel? Are you striving to be a person of excellence?

5. What does it mean to be teachable? Are you cultivating a teachable spirit?

6. What are the obstacles to teachability?

Chapter 7 The Coat of Blood

1. What is significant about Josephs brothers covering his coat in blood?

2. What does the Jewish Feast of Atonement teach us about our salvation through Christ?

3. What are the eleven results of the blood sacrifice of Jesus found in the scriptures listed in the chapter?

4. Why is it so important to preach the blood of the cross?

5. Why is singing about the blood of Jesus such a vital part of modern worship?

Chapter 8 The Anointing

1. What is the Greek word for "gifts" used in the New Testament? What does that word literally mean?

2. What is the dual flow of grace which is produced by a believer who function in the anointing they have been given? Are you holding back the flow of grace by sitting on your gifts?

3. What are the five truths about grifts listed in the chapter? Which truth are you struggling most within this season of your life?

4. The word "service" has the connotation of a waiter waiting tables. Jesus said that He came to "be waited on, but rather to wait on tables." What is the table you have been called to wait on I this season of your life?

5. Have you discovered the "because" of your life? What is it, and how are you fulfilling that aim?

Chapter 9 Things I've Learned About the Anointing

1. Who is the source of the believers anointing?

2. Scripture states that the Holy Spirit stirred Samson. Have you ever felt the stirring of the Holy Spirit, what did He move you do?

3. How did Samson's life of compromise affect his anointing?

4. Why won't God anoint the flesh?

5. Why is the Word of God the exclusive message which the Holy Spirit will anoint?

Chapter 10 Joseph a Type of Christ

1. What is a "type"?

2. How is Joseph a type of the perfection of Christ's life?

3. What are some of the similarities between Joseph and Jesus? What do they teach us about Jesus?

4. How do Josephs word "I Will Go" foreshadow the coming of Christ?

5. How are men today still trying to strip Christ of his coat, as Josephs brothers did to him?

6. Jacobs presumption that his son was dead, typifies the death and burial of Christ. The discovery that Joseph was alive typifies the resurrection of Christ. What difference does it make if Jesus raised from the dead or not?

Chapter 11 A Call To Action

1. Who is the Millennial Generation?

2. Why is the Millennial Generation so crucial for the church?

3. What are some ways we can respond to the spiritual needs of the Millennial Generation?

4. What is the importance of having a mentor? Have you sought out a mentor or spiritual father to impart wisdom into your life?

5. If you are in the position to be a mentor or spiritual father, have you embraced your calling and responsibly to the generation following you?

Contact the Author

C. Isaac De Los Santos
P.O. Box 126
Kenedy TX 78119

www.isaacdelossantos.com

Find me on Facebook @pastorisaacdelossantos

www.ingramcontent.com/pod-product-compliance
Lightning Source LLC
Chambersburg PA
CBHW060320050426
42449CB00011B/2574